COGNITIVE BEHAVIORAL THERAPY

Retrain Your Brain to Get Freedom From Anxiety,
Depression, Fear, and Negative Thoughts

IAN WILSON

TABLE OF CONTENTS

INTRODUCTION

We have all had that feeling of being stuck in our own head and often that headspace is not really a great place to be. The internal dialogue we continuously have with ourselves means we inevitably get caught up in the "what-ifs," "whys," "maybes" and even the "should haves" which can leave us feeling tremendously negative and hopeless. It can start a cycle of negativity that can be difficult to break out of, especially if we feel like we are ill-equipped to deal with it. We can often feel very alone when trying to deal with our struggles, but recognizing that we need help is the first step towards making positive changes in our lives. Cognitive Behavioral Therapy helps you to retrain the little voice inside your head to start thinking more positively and deal with those thoughts that creep in by using tools that create new ways of thinking about and understanding the challenges you are facing.

For the last few years, there has been a greater focus on mental health and the importance of ensuring that our mental well-being takes center stage. Although there has previously been a stigma associated with seeking help for mental health, it is slowly becoming more mainstream and acceptable to seek treatment and actively work on improving mental health. If we are unable to function optimally, we are unable to live our lives to the fullest. There are many tools, techniques and models that are available that tackle a variety of different mental health issues. This ebook looks at Cognitive Behavioral Therapy (CBT) as a technique for dealing with a variety of different challenges and disorders, with simple explanations and tools that you can implement to start improving on your mental health challenges.

So what exactly is CBT? CBT is a technique that helps you to understand all the underlying thoughts and feelings that lead to particular behaviors. By helping you to get an understanding of what is driving those particular behaviors, you can begin to work on changing your thoughts and feelings about them and developing new and better coping mechanisms and techniques. Many of the things we believe to be true are deeply rooted in the attitudes and beliefs we have formed throughout our lives. These beliefs can stem from our early childhood, and include things we may not have even been aware of, or beliefs that we have developed throughout our lives. While some of these may be correct, the ones that lead to the negative attitudes and behaviors we are trying to change, are the ones that we need to start working on. CBT uses different tools and techniques to help you start rethinking about those cognitive behaviors, or core beliefs, differently. The ultimate goal is to reprogram your brain to start forming new and better attitudes and beliefs that will assist you in making positive changes in your life.

CBT focuses primarily on a combination of three different things: your brain and how and why it thinks the way that it does, the things that you do and the actions that you take and finally, and your emotions. Your brain has developed specific ways of thinking over many years, often pre-programmed by the things you were exposed to from when you were a child or consistently experienced in your everyday life. We often take these beliefs and ways of thinking as foundations for taking certain actions or underlying causes of specific behaviors. Sometimes we even justify that our behavior is fine because our brain tells us that it is based on everything we learned before. Once we have taken those actions, the way that we feel quietly bubbles underneath. Depending on what those feelings are, they can have both a positive and negative impact. If you are constantly feeling negative and like you are a failure, this will influence your actions and behavior in a negative way and may hold you back from achieving great things. However, if you are able to control and influence your feelings and change them into something positive like feeling calm and in control, this can have a great positive effect on your ability to cope and how you are able to handle the situations that you are faced with.

CBT has great results when you have a particular focus area or goal that you want to achieve. It works well to tackle specific issues, and because you are using it to understand your particular way of thinking, it can often spill over and positively affect other areas of your life. You can use it for short-term goals, when there is something you are struggling with currently, or use it on an ongoing basis to make sure that you are not falling back into old bad habits and keeping your mental health challenges in check. The tools and techniques that are explained in this ebook are simple and easy to understand, which means no complicated medical or psychology terminology. Instead, it will leave you with concrete examples of things you can practice easily in your everyday life to help you understand all that you are struggling with.

Many people deal with aspects of anxiety, depression, stress and a general feeling of negativity, especially during times of change or uncertainty. Even in their mildest forms, these can have a significant impact on the quality of your daily life. It could be that you're a bit more irritated with your kids, spouse, or parents. Maybe you have that dreaded feeling of getting out of bed in the morning, which means you start out your day running late, making you tired and moody as a result.

Perhaps you're starting to realize that you can't make it through the day without finishing a bottle of wine or a six-pack to unwind before you can get to sleep. Even exercise, sex, or eating can lead to unhealthy addictions that impact your mental well-being and ability to live with a positive mindset. A fear or phobia may be holding you back from achieving a lifelong dream or being able to join in on fun activities with friends. These are all different disorders and challenges that this ebook will unpack and help you apply CBT techniques to your life.

While you may already be familiar with some of the techniques and tools that are used in CBT, like journaling and practicing mindfulness, there are many more that this ebook will explain, including Cognitive Restructuring, Situation Exposure, Behavioral Experiments and Thought Records. Each of these tools and techniques can be used for a specific purpose, with the desired outcome linked to the particular attitude, belief, or disorder that you want to change. Being able to have practical tools at your disposal that are easy to use and simple to understand can help you to start making positive changes in your life. While the names of the various tools and techniques may sound complicated, this ebook will explain the different practices in simple and easy to understand language, with practical examples of how you can put these techniques into daily use.

The CBT practices explained in this ebook will help guide you in finding practical ways to manage some of the challenges you may be facing. You may or may not already be seeing a therapist or receiving some professional help to deal and help manage a mental health issue. This ebook is not a replacement for professional medical care, but rather a supplementary guide to help you with additional tools, techniques and coping mechanisms. Many individuals with bad habits, behaviors, attitudes and mild disorders can benefit from using CBT on its own as a starting point. This ebook will also provide some guidance on when and if you should seek additional professional assistance. Let's get started on our journey through CBT!

CHAPTER 1
WHAT IS COGNITIVE BEHAVIORAL THERAPY AND HOW DOES IT WORK?

Invented in 1960 by psychiatrist Aaron Beck, Cognitive Behavioral Therapy has gained in popularity over recent years due to the fact that the tools and techniques can be used by a person on their own or together with a therapist to assist in treating a variety of disorders (Martin & Read, 2016). Through treating his patients, Dr. Beck realized that patients had an internal dialogue, that little inner voice that would influence their feelings and behaviors. Patients wouldn't often share everything that went on inside their heads with their therapist, which prompted Dr. Beck to explore the connection between thoughts and feelings. He invented the term "Automatic Thoughts" which describes the things that we think that pop into our heads automatically and give rise to certain emotions and feelings. Often these thoughts are not helpful and generally express a negative emotion coming from previous learned behaviors, which lead to unrealistic notions of what we believe to be true. We then act on these thoughts and feelings without really understanding where they are coming from or the effects they are having.

Cognitive Behavioral Therapy uses the word "cognitive" to describe the importance of our thinking and behavior to include the various techniques that are used in this kind of therapy to tackle various disorders. The ultimate goal of CBT is to identify the negative thoughts that influence us, understand why we think those things, and then use techniques to challenge the basis for those thoughts and replace them with better, more positive ways of thinking. This ultimately leads us to making better decisions and acting in a more positive way, without being held back by the fear and power the previous negative thoughts held over us.

Different Types of CBT

There are a few different types of Cognitive Behavioral Therapies, each of them sharing the same underlying premise of the connection between our thoughts and feelings and how those influence our attitudes and behaviors (Williams & Garland, 2002). Many of them share similar techniques and range from being used in a structured professional therapy setting or can be used on your own as more of a self-help program. Some of these focus specifically on the link between thoughts, feelings, and behavior; while others look at external factors in our environment that influence us. Each type has different tools and techniques that are used to tackle the particular aspect it focuses on. Sometimes there may be some overlap between these different techniques and interventions, and you can choose to use a combination of techniques for your specific issue.

- Cognitive Therapy focuses specifically on understanding what your thinking patterns are and how to change them. Often particular thinking patterns are quite destructive and inaccurate, and lead to undesirable emotions and behaviors.
- Dialectical Behavior Therapy uses mindfulness and emotional regulation to understand thoughts and behaviors.
- Multimodal Therapy is underpinned by the theory that seven different modalities (attributes or states of being) are used interconnectedly, mainly sensation, behavior, cognition, interpersonal factors, affect, imagery, and biological considerations.
- Rational Emotive Behavioral Therapy, very similar to Cognitive Therapy, seeks to identify and understand what is behind irrational beliefs and thoughts, question these beliefs and ultimately change them.

All of these have different approaches to their particular ways of therapy, but all include the same underlying strategy of changed thoughts and beliefs can lead to changed behaviors.

What Disorders Can CBT Treat?

CBT can be used to help with many different disorders and problems. Many people choose to use it as you can see results fairly quickly and the tools and techniques are easy to put into practice. The techniques are fairly structured, which means it can help you easily identify specific challenges, giving you tools to use almost immediately to develop coping strategies in less time than other traditional psychological treatments and therapies. These structured kinds of techniques can help keep you focused on what it is you are trying to change and provide you with a roadmap to clearly define the goals and outcomes you are working towards. CBT works to assist you in getting a better understanding of negative and inaccurate thinking and help give you tools so you can deal with these challenges in a better, more positive way (*The American Institute for Cognitive Therapy - Home*, 2009).

Ultimately, this kind of treatment works best when you are trying to work towards specific goals or changes in behaviors. Your goals can be specific actions, feelings or ways of dealing with particular kinds of thinking or physical issues. A specific action might include: smoking less, being more social, or learning a new skill. The feelings you might want to change could be those of anxiety, shyness, fear, or anger. You could have identified a particular way of thinking you want to change, like problem-solving or low self-esteem. CBT can even work for overcoming physical or medical problems if you have identified that a particular kind of chronic pain is an issue or perhaps having the courage to follow a treatment plan based on a diagnosis is presenting as a challenge. CBT works for a multitude of problems, all you have to do is decide what it is you want to work on and change.

You may not have a specific disorder that you want to address, but rather general emotional challenges or negativity. CBT can be very useful for dealing with these particular challenges:

- General negativity
- Managing emotions
- Relationship conflicts
- Poor communication skills
- Coping with stress
- Preventing relapse
- Grief or loss
- Mood swings
- Difficulty sleeping
- Emotional trauma due to abuse

The techniques used in CBT are very focused and goal-orientated, which means they can be used successfully to help treat a variety of recognized disorders such as:

- Anxiety and panic attacks
- Stress
- Depression

- Fear and phobias
- Addiction and eating disorders
- Anger issues
- Obsessive Compulsive Disorder (OCD)
- Post-Traumatic Stress Disorder (PTSD)

CBT can have a lasting positive impact in the management and understanding of these challenges and disorders and can be even more effective when used together with other treatments recommended by your health care professional.

How Does CBT Work?

Your thoughts and feelings impact your behavior and attitude, whether you understand it or are aware of it or not. If deep down you believe that you are a terrible cook, because once when you were little you burnt a piece of toast and your mother made a big deal about it, you may have always played safe by not trying to cook anything new because you believe that you can't do it. This may have impacted your relationships or even job prospects, if you always wanted to do something, but believed that you couldn't. That little voice inside our heads directs the choices, feelings, and emotions that we have every day. The confidence to wear those bright shoes, start a conversation with a stranger, or even say yes to that big project at work are all influenced by our thinking. If your thinking is always negative, you can generally expect negative outcomes. Whereas if you have a positive mindset, you are already heading in the direction to achieve positive outcomes. You may not be able to control every single little aspect of your life, but you can learn how to deal with the things that are inside your control. Learning how to take control of the things you can will help you to make positive changes by working on things bit by bit. You do not have to solve all your problems and all your negative thoughts all at once. Instead, build your confidence by starting to work on one thing and then move forward from there.

Identifying the Issue

The first thing you will need to do with CBT is to identify what it is you are struggling with and want to change. This may be the hardest part of this kind of therapy, especially if you struggle with looking at yourself in an objective manner and pin-pointing the problem and pain areas. This will require a lot of introspection and honesty with yourself. The reality is, if you are ignoring something that is or may be a problem in the future, you will stay in the same negative cycle. Look at the things that are happening in your life. Which things are you struggling with or are causing conflict or difficulties? Are there specific relationships that are strained with a partner, parent, child, colleague, or friend? Do you have fears that manifest negatively in other places in your life? Once you have identified the exact things you need to work on, you can start using the relevant techniques that will help you develop coping strategies moving forward. A major benefit of CBT is that it enables you to implement the techniques you have learned with your present situation and apply it to them in the future.

Being committed to work on the techniques and tools you learn through CBT will determine whether or not it will ultimately work for you. Are you committed to making positive changes in your life? Will you stick with the techniques and tools to work toward the goals you have set for yourself? Just like all things in your life, you need to stick with something in order to see results.

The next step in the process of CBT is to identify what the thoughts and feelings are that are driving these negative behaviors, emotional challenges, and specific disorders you want to change. By understanding those thoughts and feelings and where they come from, you can start to understand the impact that they are having in your life (Richards, n.d.). You may need to talk with someone or write this down as you explore and identify those feelings. You will need to think about how particular situations make you feel, what you experience, and what you think about them. You will need to identify how you are interpreting a situation, person, or event and what your beliefs are about this particular instance. Sometimes our beliefs around a particular thing can be so ingrained, that we are unable to see past our already pre-conceived interpretations and may need someone who is neutral to help us identify irrational, illogical, or negative thoughts and interpretations. Although this may be a little difficult, it will be very rewarding and doing it will ensure that you get positive results from CBT.

Challenging Your Beliefs

By having a clear idea of the changes you need to make and identifying all the negative thoughts, feelings, and beliefs about that particular issue, you will use one of the specific tools and techniques in CBT to start challenging the validity and legitimacy of those thoughts and feelings and your interpretation of how it affects your behavior, as well as your interactions with others. A lot of the time, we continue engaging or disengaging in particular behaviors and feelings because we subconsciously look for things that reinforce our negative beliefs and attitudes.

Behavioral Experiments are one of the tools used in CBT which can be used to challenge some of these beliefs and thoughts (Patterson, 2006). The way it works is that you start looking for specific things that either reinforce and support that particular belief or provide information that helps prove the inaccuracy of that belief. For example, you might believe that you are not a smart person because you are unable to engage in a conversation on a particular topic or feel like you lack the ability to complete or follow through on tasks because you are easily distracted. In order to unpack that belief, you need to look at all the evidence that will show it to be either true or untrue. What makes a person smart? Is it finishing school or getting a degree? It could be the ability to problem solve and apply the things you learn every day to manage daily challenges you face. When you look at the evidence and see that you have, in fact, gotten a high school diploma and were accepted into college or university, that is indisputable evidence that you are smart. So, believing that you are not smart is untrue and inaccurate. If you begin listing all of the things that you do every day, you will probably find a whole list of things that you finish and accomplish daily and, therefore, the belief that you are unable to complete tasks is also inaccurate and untrue.

Thought Records are another powerful way of looking at whether your thoughts and feelings about a particular person or situation is valid. For example, if your boss tells you that you are not good at your job, before you start just believing that to be true, you need to find all the evidence that may prove this statement to be inaccurate or prove it to be correct. Your boss may have given you a big project to work on the previous week, or leave you to work independently for the majority of the time and allow you to make decisions that impact your daily work. If they really believed you were not good at your job, they wouldn't have done those things, would they? By being able to look at the situation honestly and balancing all the facts, you will be able to see a more balanced and accurate view on the thought and a situation in particular.

Behavioral Experiments help people understand their feelings and emotions about particular instances, whereas Thought Records provide more practical insight into specific occurrences (Martin & Read, 2016). These methods can be used for many beliefs that we hold to be true, and taking an objective and methodical approach in finding evidence to the contrary can help you with creating better self-esteem and give you the courage to pursue the things that you have held back from doing because your feelings and attitudes were based on an inaccurate perception. Sometimes the things we hold to be true are only true to us because we give them that power or we hold a particular person's opinion in such high regard that we never challenge the validity of their claims. You may have avoided activities or situations because you didn't believe that you could do them or you had a negative association based on the assumption of what you thought you could or could not do. Once you start seeing how many of those beliefs are inaccurate, you can start engaging in activities that you previously held back from and create new positive belief structures that are empowering.

Creating New Behaviors

Once you have started to dismantle those negative and inaccurate belief systems, you can begin using other tools and techniques in CBT to develop new positive behaviors and regulate negative thoughts through activities designed to help you with the challenge or disorder you are struggling with (Serio, 2019).

The important thing is to now move forward with a specific goal you have in mind so you have a better picture and idea of all the things you are setting out to achieve and are able to measure progress against the milestones you have set. If you are trying to overcome a particular fear, for example, using the Situation Exposure technique in CBT can help move you closer to getting over that fear or building a tolerance toward that by gradually increasing exposure to that particular fear. This can help greatly with anxiety as by starting out with small exposure activities you can tackle each instance individually and gradually build up to bigger exposures. By overcoming small tasks one at a time, you also help to build self-confidence.

Sometimes we are so stressed or depressed or caught up in our own heads with all those negative thoughts, feelings and beliefs, that we shy away or deliberately avoid activities that bring us joy. Pleasant Activity Scheduling can help create balance and keep you motivated by ensuring that you make time to do things that are enjoyable or that you wouldn't ordinarily do. It can also be used as a reward technique for accomplishing tasks which may feel challenging or you have avoided due to those negative thoughts and beliefs. Even if it is just one thing a day, you will feel a sense of achievement because you have completed a task that you set out to do, even if it was the fun and enjoyable one.

Mindfulness and meditation are powerful tools used in CBT. They will help you find calm in the chaos, regulate your emotions, and bring you back into a positive mindset to tackle the challenges ahead of you. They can also provide a space to focus on something else, rather than the particular situation or negative emotion you may be feeling at the time. You can collect your thoughts and refocus on positivity in order to get back on track.

Benefits of CBT

Once you get started you will be pleasantly surprised at the many benefits you gain in your everyday life. The entire process of CBT is to fundamentally change the negative inner voice fueled by inaccurate or debilitating thoughts and beliefs into a more positive and encouraging mindset. This change will inevitably automatically and gradually start to influence how you see the world around you and yourself. Instead of being filled with dread and negativity, you may find it replaced with openness and optimism. Instead of avoiding particular activities, you may find yourself more inclined to try something new (*7 Benefits of Cognitive Behavioral Therapy | CCPS*, 2015).

You will notice you are worrying less about a particular event or outcome because you have learned to understand where those thoughts are coming from and have the ability to rationalize them. The old habit of perpetually playing the same mistake over and over will dissipate as you learn new coping skills and start breaking the cycle of negative thinking patterns.

Learning how to cope and manage stress becomes second nature as you acquire tools to discern between whether something requires you to actively engage in fixing that particular problem, or if you need to take a break and step away to get clarity and calm in a situation. This leads to fewer emotional outbursts and better emotional regulation.

When you have tools, a goal and a plan for achieving that goal, you are more likely to be productive and less likely to procrastinate. Having a clear idea of what it is you want to do and setting aside the negative beliefs that have stopped you before, means that you feel better about doing the things you set your mind to, instead of allowing yourself to talk yourself out of doing it.

As we learn to understand and interpret our inner voice and become able to discern and dissect negative thinking patterns and where they come from, ultimately leads to having a more positive outlook on life, improved communication and relationships, and higher self-esteem.

CHAPTER 2
PRACTICAL USES OF CBT IN EVERYDAY LIFE

CBT can be used to tackle a variety of disorders through the breadth of techniques used in this kind of therapy. However, these same techniques can be used in your everyday life to help overcome general feelings of negativity and increase your emotional well-being. We often get so busy living life, with all the demands that are placed on us, we very rarely stop to think about whether we are actually coping emotionally or if we are being held back somewhat by negative beliefs, thoughts, and behaviors. By understanding how the different techniques work, you can use these to start seeing remarkable improvements in your life on a daily basis.

While you may think that you are coping well, the easiest way to tell if you need to re-evaluate how you are dealing with things is to identify whenever you have an overly strong emotional reaction to something or are triggered by a particular person, place, or thing that results in an undesirable response. If you feel like you are coping fine, but all it takes is one thing to set you off, you start taking a deeper look at the underlying reason behind it. You may think that it is perfectly reasonable to get upset when a friend doesn't respond to a text within a certain time frame,, but if you take the time to examine and understand the reason that you got upset and where your response is actually justifiable, you may uncover deeper emotional thoughts and beliefs that are linked to this reaction. By using CBT techniques to learn how to identify what these triggers are, you will find yourself much more even tempered, having a more positive outlook on life, and being able to handle situations that may have previously triggered negative reactions, behaviors, and emotional responses.

Overcoming Negativity and Emotional Responses Through Cognitive Restructuring

A core technique in CBT is Cognitive Restructuring. This technique is concerned with understanding our thoughts about the things that happen to us and how we respond to them. It is about retraining our brains to respond to things differently. Just like learning to do anything, practice and consistency are key. Cognitive Restructuring is an ongoing process that you need to be aware of and keep doing all the time. You can get better at doing something if you do it repeatedly. Every time you recognize that you have an emotional or negative response to something, that is when you need to start looking at where it is coming from and why it is influencing your behavior in that way (Serio, 2019).

Stop and Reflect on the Situation

Cognitive Restructuring can be very effective when you use this technique as soon as you realize that you are having a strong negative or emotional response to a situation. It may be a one-off occurrence where the techniques can be used to help bring you back into the present and create distance from the response or situation, but it can also be used to identify situations when you continuously have the same negative or emotional response to a certain feeling, activity, or situation. Do you have the same emotional or negative response whenever you feel stressed? Perhaps you always need or crave that beer or glass of wine whenever you feel stressed or overwhelmed. If you are feeling especially anxious, do you want to hide away, avoid certain people, or make excuses so you don't have to take part in activities? When feeling angry, do you lash out verbally or even in a violent way, taking out your anger and frustration on people or objects around you? As soon as you start recognizing overly emotional responses to situations or people, you need to take a moment to stop what you are doing and reflect on the situation. As soon as you notice your response, pause. By taking the time to stop and think about your response, you immediately give yourself an opportunity to recognize the situation and the attached response and start looking at it in a way to try and understand the response, rather than getting drawn into the emotional fall-out (Patterson, 2006).

Identifying Triggers

Once you have taken a step back from your emotional response, you can identify the trigger that led you to respond in that way. Triggers are things that can happen in our external or internal environment that start you on a particular path of action in response to what happened. External triggers can be caused by things that happen or something that someone has said, whether it is a car cutting in front of you in rush hour traffic, or a comment from your spouse. Internal triggers happen inside our heads, like being reminded of a particular event that had an impact on us, such as losing a loved one. Or, it can be a thought that pops into our heads, like something we wanted to say during a meeting but forgot.

If you can identify the trigger that leads to the overly emotional response, you can start to understand why it is that the trigger caused you to react in that way. Remember, the point of CBT is to identify and understand the root cause of our behaviors and start reprogramming our brains to respond differently (Patterson, 2006).

You may not even be aware that something is a trigger and thought that maybe you were just in a hurry when the car cut you off, so that is why you reacted in the way that you did. It is important, once you realize that you've responded in an overly emotional or negative way, to step back and pinpoint the trigger that perhaps caused it. An easy way to identify the trigger is to take a "who, what, where, when" approach that will help you understand the "why." Recognizing triggers present at the time of the emotional or negative reaction can help you highlight where the real issue is so you can deal with it appropriately.

Who was with you at the time? Think about the particular situation and whether there was a person who was a part of it. As we are social creatures, people spend a lot of time with others and are emotionally influenced by those we share time and space with, whether frequently, infrequently, or just in passing.

What actually happened? If you walk through the situation and replay the events, you can try and understand the sequence of what really happened. Try to recall all the details, both big and small. Sometimes the smallest detail is the thing that we may have missed and may, in fact, be the trigger that caused the response. We often think that it is the biggest thing that happened that caused us to react in a certain way, but often it is something we initially thought to be insignificant that is causing our distress.

When did you start having the negative or emotional response? Looking at the timeline of the events can help you understand where the issue really started and is particularly important if you are trying to understand things a day or two after the event occurred. You are not trying to pinpoint when the final emotional or negative response happened, but rather when you first became aware that something was upsetting you or affecting you. It is in those early moments that your trigger may have appeared.

Where did it happen? A lot of our emotional responses and feelings can be linked to particular places where something may have happened before or to a certain memory that you may have. Returning to your childhood home where you may have had previous negative experiences can often trigger an emotional or negative response to an entirely different situation, simply because you are in a place where there are a lot of memories.

Becoming Aware of Automatic Thoughts

Automatic thoughts are the things that we think about inside our heads, that we are often not even aware of. They are the little voices inside your head that automatically ask "What does she want now?" when you see an email from your boss in your inbox, or that immediate thought of, "What an idiot! Doesn't he know how to drive?" when you are cut off by yet another driver during your morning commute. It can even be a particular feeling we associate with a memory, like the smell of the ocean that reminds us of a cherished family holiday or an advertisement on television of a grandmother playing with her grandchildren that reminds you of your late grandmother. We all have these thoughts running through our heads and often we are not even sure where they come from. They spontaneously pop into our minds and invoke a certain feeling around a current situation.

When you practice Cognitive Restructuring, you need to start becoming aware of these automatic thoughts and where they are coming from, as they may be having a negative impact or be triggering how you respond in particular situations. The idea is to get a clear picture of all the things that are influencing your thinking and behavior so you can start effectively changing it (Boyes, 2012).

How Intense and Appropriate Is Your Emotional Response?

As much as we like to believe we are always correct in how we have responded to a situation, the reality is that sometimes we need to reflect on that emotional response and see if it is *actually* appropriate. Our emotions stem from what we are thinking and the intensity of those emotions is driven by the kind of thoughts and thinking patterns we engage in.

If you get cut off in traffic, you will most likely have some form of an emotional response to the situation. Opening your window to yell at the other car while honking and shouting obscenities is an emotional response that is most likely driven by your thoughts regarding the incident and perceived thoughts about the driver. The little voice inside your head says, "Can't he drive? What an inconsiderate idiot!" and you feel angry or have intense feelings of rage.

If the little voice inside your head is thinking, "Oh my goodness! He could have hit me and caused an accident!" your reaction is more likely one of fear and anxiety about what might have happened in the situation. You may also feel more than one emotion or have a few different thoughts regarding the situation, like anger *and* anxiety, which would be common in this kind of situation.

Once you identify all the different emotions you felt in the particular situation based on your response and your reaction, you can rate your responses and emotions on a scale of 1 to 10. The lower end of the scale being small and mild, while the higher end being extreme and more intense.

Creating Alternative Thoughts and Thinking

Now that you have stopped to reflect on your negative response, identified the triggers and the automatic thoughts in that situation, and have rated the intensity and appropriateness of the response, you can start creating alternative thoughts around the situation. Remember, we are trying to reprogram our brains with Cognitive Restructuring, which means we will be coming up with different positive thoughts for the same situation (Legg, 2020).

If we think about the driver who cut you off in traffic, instead of thinking, "He could have hit me or caused an accident!" you can try and come up with an alternative thought to the situation like, "That could have ended badly, but I was paying attention because I am a good driver and managed to handle the situation well." Instead of: "Can't he drive? What an inconsiderate idiot!" you could change it to: "He seems to be in a hurry, perhaps there is a family emergency he needs to deal with."

The reality is that there are many reasons why things happen the way that they do and a slew of factors that can impact a situation. You need to be flexible in your thinking to start considering all the other alternatives that might be just as valid as the automatic thought you have in your head. It is only by being open to alternatives and looking at different perspectives to the same situations that you can start challenging your own negative thoughts and learn to manage your emotional response better. By being open to different thoughts, you are also able to see more clearly how the situation played out, thereby giving you a much more realistic view of an event. Things are not always as we perceive them to be at first glance, and only if we take a step back and consider alternatives with an open mind are we able to see the bigger picture.

Reevaluate Your Emotional Response

After looking at the whole situation and coming up with alternative thoughts regarding the situation, you need to go back to your original rating and see if it is fair and correct based on the new thoughts you have introduced to the equation. It is this practice of questioning and reevaluating that will help you change and develop better habits and fine-tune your automatic thinking for future situations. Understanding why your initial response may have been overly emotional or negative and deconstructing it so you feel less negative, will help you reinforce this technique because you have been able to change your emotional response for the better.

Creating Thought Records for Cognitive Restructuring

The technique outlined above is quite easy to follow and implement in your daily life. Using Thought Records can be a very useful template to use for everything you are working through and dealing with. They also serve as a physical record you can refer back to and work on retrospectively. A Thought Record can be a journal, Word document, the note section on your phone, or any app or program you can write in, so that you can follow the steps and document everything as you go along.

Start out by listing the different stages of Cognitive Restructuring as discussed in detail above:

- Stop and Reflect
- Identify Triggers (who, what, when, where)
- Automatic Thoughts
- First Intensity Rating
- Alternative Thoughts
- Reevaluate Intensity Rating

When you encounter a situation where you have an emotionally intense or negative reaction to, open your book or digital notepad and work through the list above for that situation. You can also use this for past situations or specific instances where you are particularly struggling. The purpose is to have a physical record of your thoughts and use the technique to work through them in a logical manner to create understanding and recreate new thoughts.

After doing this for a little while, working through the Cognitive Restructuring steps will become easier and more natural. Eventually you won't even need to prompt yourself to think about it; you will be able to do it all in your head and manage negative thoughts and emotional responses much more quickly. It will also help you to identify common automatic thoughts and themes so you can focus on them to lessen their impact.

Remember that CBT and techniques like Cognitive Restructuring are not a "one-off-cure-all." These skills require ongoing practice, evaluation and change. You can't expect work through one exercise for a situation where you felt angry or very anxious and then expect that you will magically be fine the next time it happens. You need to work on it consistently and frequently. It is a new skill you are learning and training your brain to do, so you have to keep at it (Boyes, 2012). It can feel a bit overwhelming and daunting in the beginning, but as you start practicing more regularly, you will see the positive effects, which will motivate you to keep going. Remember that you can also reach out to a therapist or other professional support to work through these techniques with you, even a trusted friend can provide invaluable support.

CHAPTER 3
MANAGING ANXIETY

CBT has been used to successfully tackle a variety of disorders, including anxiety and anxiety related conditions. For many people, anxiety can be extremely debilitating. Luckily, the techniques used in CBT can address the different ways anxiety manifests daily and ultimately lead to an improved quality of life. The techniques used focus on the underlying premise that by changing your negative thoughts and beliefs, you can change your emotional and physical responses and behaviors. Anxiety can be exhausting and affect all parts of a person's life, but there is hope. Through therapy, you can work through the underlying causes and issues rather than simply treating the symptoms with medication. Life can be better and things can change positively.

There are many different kinds of anxiety disorders including panic disorders, social anxiety, and generalized anxiety, Post-Traumatic Stress Disorder (PTSD) and Obsessive Compulsive Disorder (OCD) (Brundt, 2019). The type and length of the therapy you might require will be dependent on how long you have been suffering from the specific anxiety disorder, and how severe and debilitating it is. CBT techniques use an approach that is focused on the here and now, looking at the current situation and understanding the feelings and beliefs that are causing the reaction. CBT then seeks to find better ways to manage and change those behaviors.

Challenging Your Thoughts

The thoughts you have about a situation can strongly influence how you perceive the reality of a situation, rather than the actual happenings of the situation itself. Sometimes you can get so worked up in your own head about something that is *going* to happen, that it can negatively influence how you respond or cause you to avoid it all together. Every situation that happens can have various emotions attached to it, and the emotions affect your response and behavior in that situation. Sometimes those emotions are automatic as they are based on previous experiences or perceptions, which is why CBT works at challenging those thoughts and emotions in order to have a more realistic view of the situation and possible outcomes (Cuncic, 2020).

The previous chapter explores Cognitive Restructuring in depth and those tools can be used very effectively for treating anxiety, too. Being able to identify your negative thoughts and emotions and then replacing them with positive and more realistic thoughts and emotions about a situation will greatly improve your emotional well-being and ability to handle future situations. Always remember that what is going on inside your head is often coming from a place of fear and is most often not a true representation of what is happening in real life.

The first step is to identify the negative thoughts you are having about the situation. As soon as you start feeling fearful, anxious, or nervous, stop and think about why it is you are feeling that way. Try and identify all the emotions you are feeling and the thoughts that are driving those emotions. Being excruciatingly honest with yourself is crucial. You must accept that you need to unpack all the thoughts and emotions you are having, however rational or irrational they might be. You want to get a clear picture of what it is that is driving your fear and anxiety.

Once you are aware of your thoughts and feelings about the situation, you need to look at them rationally and see if they are indeed valid or not. This means considering the most likely outcome as compared to the outcome your fear and anxiety are probably pushing (Kaczkurkin & Foa, 2015). This will help you deal with the outcome in a positive manner. For example, if you have been invited to a party and suffer from social anxiety, you may be fearful of meeting new people because you think that they won't like you or that you are boring and have nothing interesting to say. Think about how this would make you feel if it did actually happen. Would you be upset that people don't like you? What other things are you afraid might happen and how would that make you feel? Then think about the actual likelihood of that happening. If it is a social gathering with people that you know, they already like you because they have met you and then chose to invite you. Use the person who invited you to get a feel for the other guests. You may find out you have a lot in common with them!

You might find it helpful to make a list of all the pros and cons about the situation and how each will make you feel. Then look at the list and decide on the likelihood of those things happening. If you are anxious about tripping and falling in front of everyone when you arrive, think about the real-life odds. Has it happened before? What makes you think it will happen again? Having a more realistic view of what could feasibly occur at the party will remove some of the fear and the unknown.

The next thing you can do is replace those negative thoughts and feelings with alternatives or play through the situation in your head and use calming and reaffirming statements. For example, if you feel upset that no one will like you start reminding yourself about all the people who do indeed like you, remember you were invited to the party by someone after all. The party lasts only a few hours and there will be a flurry of people; everyone will forget about the party and who was there in a few days anyway. You will be surprised at how powerful our inner voice can be when we feed it positivity instead of negativity. Try thinking to yourself over and over again, "I am calm. It is ok if someone doesn't like me because I have friends that do."

Make a list of situations or triggers that make you feel anxious and come up with a positive saying for each of them. This will help keep you focused on a positive outcome, rather than negative one. Also, by having this list it may help you feel more prepared, like you have a plan, which is also very useful in calming your anxiety. Often our biggest fear is being in a situation when we are unprepared. Working on these things before you are in a particular situation can help you feel more in control of your thinking and the reality of what might happen instead allowing your irrational thoughts and feelings to take center stage.

Situation Exposure

Most of the time, we would rather avoid people, places, and things that make us feel fearful, anxious, or uncomfortable. It is easier to withdraw than to deal with things head-on. This can negatively impact how we enjoy life, as we may be shying away and missing out on the positive impacts of the avoided scenario. Situation Exposure or Exposure Therapy is a technique used in CBT that essentially ties in with the old adage of "facing your fears." The theory behind it is that if you have fear, anxiety, or a particular phobia, exposure to these things in incremental doses can help build a tolerance and calm your fears and anxiety (Whalley, 2019). It can be used in conjunction with Cognitive Restructuring if you are trying to challenge your beliefs using Behavioral Experiments to test whether what you believe is actually correct. The idea is to confront your fear or phobia in such a way that it does not cause an undesirable reaction or outcome. For example, if you have a fear of snakes you wouldn't start by jumping in a pen with a rattlesnake. This is too extreme to start with (not to mention dangerous). A photograph of a snake might be a better first step. It will ease your reaction because you know it is just a photograph, so nothing terrible will happen to you.

Gradually exposing yourself to non-threatening situations or things related to your phobia or anxiety is called Systematic Desensitization. The idea is to increase the intensity of the exposure bit-by-bit until you are able to function rationally and appropriately. As you start from a very low threshold, you can learn techniques to manage the fear and associated panic in small doses. Once you have mastered the first increment, you will grow in self-confidence and awareness to build up to the next exposure.

Learning relaxation and breathing techniques is incredibly valuable for any anxiety sufferer, but is especially useful before exposing yourself to your fears or phobias, so you are ready to use the calming tools when you need them. In the middle of a panic or anxiety attack, these tools will allow you to quickly refocus your mind and regulate your body back to a state of calm. There are four different tools explained at the end of this chapter, including deep breathing, visualization, muscle relaxation, and counting.

Think about what is causing you anxiety and decide on your goal. Remember to make it a realistic goal; if you are afraid of heights there is no need to make your goal sky-diving (unless it is something you really want to do). It may be as simple as traveling on the top floor of a double decker bus or climbing at a look-out point. Once you know what you are working toward, make a list of all the steps it will take to get there or particular situations that you need to expose yourself to along the way. Try to be as detailed as possible with about 10 to 20 steps, keeping in mind that small steps may be easier to overcome than giant leaps when dealing with anxiety. If you feel anxious about going to parties or places with a lot of people, start small with perhaps a picture of a crowded mall or concert, then maybe watching a video of places with lots of crowds.

You could go somewhere with only a few people that are far apart, then a place where people are closer together, before moving onto your final goal of attending that party, going to that concert, or simply visiting your local mall. Think about what will work for you and maybe ask a friend to help think of some ideas for gradual exposure if you start getting anxious just thinking about making the list.

Once you have your list of steps that you can start to take to reach your goal and overcome your particular anxieties and fears you have. Ideally you want to carry on and stay with one step until you feel comfortable enough to move onto the next one. It won't help if you haven't overcome going out to lunch with two friends in a restaurant to then jump into doing a family get-together with 20 people. When working through a particular step, you should be using the tools discussed below to help you manage your anxiety and fear in that particular situation. Ideally, the goal is to learn how to focus on moving past what you are feeling and learn that those feelings will not cause you any harm and you can teach yourself ways to make them go away. As you feel yourself getting anxious, you use the tools to calm down and manage your anxiety until you are ready to face the situation you are trying to overcome. You carry on doing this all the way through your steps until you finally reach your goal. Don't rush the process. Take as much time as you need to work through each step. If at any stage you feel that the next step is a bit of a bigger challenge, you can always move back a previous step or add in another step.

Deep Breathing Technique

You can use relaxation and breathing techniques to minimize your physical response to the situation, place or object to avoid hyperventilating or shaking uncontrollably. Learning deep breathing techniques is an invaluable tool in dealing with anxiety in general. If you are experiencing a panic attack, you tend to start taking short rapid breaths that lead to feeling dizzy, and the lack of oxygen can make you feel disorientated, which can increase your feeling of anxiety. This is caused because your body detects elevated levels of carbon-dioxide in your blood and your brain tells your body that it is in trouble and causes various physical reactions to take place, seemingly outside your control which inevitably leaves you feeling more anxious.

By taking control of your breathing, you immediately calm the body's physiological responses by giving it the oxygen it needs and are able to focus on your breathing instead of the situation or thing that is making you anxious. Pulling your focus toward your breathing will help you stay grounded, and bring you back into the present moment instead of allowing your thoughts and feelings to take control (Ankrom, 2019). You can practice deep breathing anywhere you are and it doesn't matter if you are sitting or lying down or standing up. Try to work on bringing your mind to focus completely on your breathing.

- Start by inhaling deeply through your nose for 5 seconds, keeping your shoulders and your body relaxed. If you feel yourself tensing up, roll your shoulders backwards and forwards a few times to loosen them up and allow them to relax. Breathe in deeply so your chest only rises a little and you feel your abdomen pushing out a bit as your lungs fill with air. Remember, it is your diaphragm that pushes down to allow your lungs the space to fill with air. Put your hand on your diaphragm to help feel it move as you inhale.
- Now, exhale slowly through your mouth keeping your lips slightly pursed, but not tight. Your jaw should be relaxed and your lips soft. Try to exhale slowly for 10 seconds. Focus on your breath leaving your lungs and keep it as slow as possible.
- Repeat inhaling for 5 seconds and exhaling slowly for 10 seconds as per the above steps. Carry on doing this breathing exercise until you feel calm. It helps to count the seconds in your head while you are breathing, as it gives your brain something to focus on other than why you need to be breathing to calm down in the first place (Gotter, 2018).

You may find, at first, that trying this breathing technique may even cause you a bit of anxiety to begin with. You may be feeling anxious about how you are breathing or getting the exercise right. Don't worry. Just stop for a bit and try again later or in a few days, whenever you are feeling ready. This is why it is important to learn and practice breathing techniques before you start with Exposure Therapy, as you don't want to just exchange one feeling of anxiety for another, but rather use the breathing technique as a tool to help overcome feelings of fear and anxiety in the moment when they occur.

Visualization Tool

Sometimes the best way for us to feel calm is to imagine that we are in a place that makes us feel calm. It's all about finding your "happy place." You want to take your attention away from the particular situation or object that is causing you anxiety and think about a place that makes you feel calm and relaxed instead. Your "happy place" could be a real place you have been to before or that actually exists or it can be completely imaginary. You want to pick something that isn't too complicated so you can recall quickly in future when you are in an anxious situation.

Try and think about or create all the little details for your happy place. What does it look like? Imagine the colors, sounds, and smells. Think about how this place makes you feel. You should feel calm, serene and in control. It is a relaxing place to be. You have nothing to fear in your happy place.

Once you have a good picture inside your head, whenever you are feeling anxious and fearful, close your eyes and visualize yourself in your happy place. Take slow breaths and think about how your happy place makes you feel calm and at peace, allow those positive relaxing feelings to overtake the feelings of anxiety.

Muscle Relaxation

When we start feeling anxious, our body responds by tensing up. Our muscles become hard and tight, making it hard to move freely. This muscle tension can cause headaches, and in some instances, we feel paralyzed to move because of the muscle tension. As soon as you feel your body start tensing up as your anxiety levels rise, stop and take a deep breath. Find somewhere calm and quiet where you can sit or lie down and be still, then close your eyes and concentrate completely on your breathing (Legg, 2018). Make a fist with your hands and squeeze them tightly. Hold it tightly for a few seconds and feel the muscles tense in your fists. Then slowly start opening your hands, finger by finger and feel the tension being released from your hands. You will start to feel more relaxed as your hands start opening.

Work your way up or down your body by making the different muscle groups tighten with tension and then release them again. Focus individually on your arms, shoulders, legs and feet, and continue the process of tension and release until you start to feel your entire body relax and let go of the tension and anxiety. Focusing on how your body is physically responding to your feelings of anxiety and using the muscle relaxation technique to regain control and release those feelings gives your mind something else to concentrate on instead of the anxiety.

Counting to Calm

Counting can be a very effective and simple tool to help you to refocus your mind on something other than your anxious feelings. Depending on how high your levels of anxiety are, it can offer relief fairly quickly or it can take a little longer. Luckily, there is no limit on how high you can count, so keep going until you feel calmer. As soon as you find yourself feeling anxious, close your eyes and move away to a quiet space if you are able. Then simply start counting slowly, starting from one. This can be very effective and useful when you are in busy crowded spaces and it may not be easy to use some of the other calming techniques.

CHAPTER 4
MANAGING STRESS

Stress is something that we all deal with every day. It has almost become part of our daily lives and seems to be a constant companion as we try to juggle life and all the challenges that come along with it. Whether it is a demanding job with an overbearing boss and constant looming deadlines, a household filled with children and chores or those financial worries that keep you up at night, each of us has different levels of stress in one or many different parts of our lives. For the most part, some of us might seemingly be coping and for others it is a daily battle to keep stress levels low enough in order to function properly. Unfortunately, sometimes those stress levels can boil over and have an effect on how you function or your emotional response to a situation. I am sure you can relate to feeling like you may have overreacted in response to something because you were stressed about something else entirely unrelated.

Using CBT for the treatment of stress and using it to lower stress levels is based on the same theory as the foundation for all other CBT interventions, that thoughts influence our feelings, emotions and behaviors (Koeck, 2015). Changing these thoughts from a negative to a positive can improve how we deal with situations. Constantly thinking negative thoughts or worrying about negative outcomes immediately puts you in a negative headspace. Even if you aren't actively thinking negative thoughts, the underlying negative beliefs you hold onto significantly impact your mood and your stress levels. If in the back of your mind you are constantly worried about whether you will have enough money to get to your next payday, it will subconsciously influence how you feel and your responses to anything that is related to money or spending money. You might find grocery shopping to be a very stressful experience because you spend the entire time worrying about how much you will be spending because of your underlying belief that you will not have enough money to last you until payday. The goal of Cognitive Behavior Therapy is to enable you to identify and replace the negative thought with a positive thought. You will become aware of the specific negative thought that is causing you to feel worried and stressed, and will be able to actively talk yourself down with a realistic positive thought. If you put together a budget and know that if you stick to your grocery list, you will have enough to last you until payday, you can replace the negative thought with one that is positive; like reminding yourself that you have a budget and you are very good at sticking to a plan. You could also look back at past experience to see if you have a realistic worry or expectation. If you have always managed to have enough money to last you until the end of the month and nothing has changed with your spending habits and expenses this particular month, there is a very good chance that the outcome will be the same, which means you have nothing to worry about.

Using CBT techniques can help you retrain your brain into learning new patterns of thinking to better cope with stressful situations. You can use the techniques in order to identify and understand which particular things are causing you stress in your life and how to manage those influences better. As you start to use the techniques and see improvement, it will lead to building better self-confidence enabling you to feel more confident in being able to handle future stressful situations better.

Different Causes of Stress

Stress can manifest in many different ways, and can be influenced by internal and external factors. Sometimes these stressors may seem small and insignificant, but are having a measurable impact on your life. Being able to identify what these stressors are and developing techniques to help manage and cope better will help you see a positive change in your daily life. CBT can work on a number of common and prevalent stressful situations such as:

- Relationship challenges can extend beyond a spouse or partner and include relationships with family members and friends. Often there may be a particular relationship with someone that is causing stress.
- Career or business stress is quite common, as you spend a large part of your day working or at the office. Sometimes the desire to succeed and do well at your job or own business can cause you stress. You may be unhappy, overworked or feel underappreciated.
- Stress around major life changes and events is especially common. Moving, going to college, getting married or divorced, having children and grieving a death or a loss are all big life changes and come with a lot of uncertainty that causes stress.
- Traumatic events can cause stress that can be ongoing as you may find yourself reliving that particular moment or constantly over-analyzing what happened. Sometimes you might feel fine a few weeks or months after something traumatic has happened

and then all of a sudden have an emotional outburst or reaction that is seemingly unrelated, but is caused by the underlying stress of what happened.

- Feeling stressed for no apparent reason when on the surface everything seems fine and you should be coping well, can, in itself, cause stress. When everything seems to be going well and you can't help wondering why you are feeling stressed when you have no reason to, means that there may be an underlying cause or negative thinking that is contributing to your stress.

- Having low levels of self-esteem or self-confidence can cause stress because you are constantly dealing with feelings of inadequacy or potential failure. Stress caused by this tends to hold us back from pursuing and achieving certain activities, life changes or achievements.

- Sometimes stress can be caused by particular activities or actions. You may feel stressed about having to exercise or going out to a party. These activities can be one off things that may cause you stress or something that is ongoing and you need to engage in daily so finding a way to cope is very important.

- External factors which are outside of your control that may or may not have a direct influence or impact such as environmental issues like global warming, politics, pandemics or disease outbreaks and world financial markets can also cause stress for some individuals.

The different causes of stress can be both inside and outside of your control. Sometimes we have no choice but to be exposed to particular situations, people and activities so we need to learn tools and techniques to manage our stress both while we are in those particular situations and afterwards to make sure that it does not have a major negative impact in our daily lives.

Tools for Dealing With Stress

With so many different things causing stress in our daily lives, it is no wonder that many of us struggle to make it through a day without feeling like we've been hit by a train by the time we get into bed. Feeling overwhelmed and constantly pushed to your limits can make you feel tired and unmotivated which will have a significant impact on your quality of life. You may avoid activities that you enjoy because you feel like you don't have the energy, or tell yourself you don't have time because you need to focus on something else that is causing you stress. CBT offers a variety of tools to help you understand and manage your stress, which can be used together or you can use whichever individual tool is best suited to the particular stressful situation you are dealing with (Gregoire, 2013).

Planning and Prioritization

One of the biggest influences on our stress levels is that we feel we have a multitude of activities, tasks, deadlines and responsibilities that all need to happen immediately. You may have a growing list of things inside your head that you know you need to do and the thought of all of these things is causing you to become stressed and agitated. On your growing list, you may think that each one is as important as the next or that you will be able to accomplish all of these things in the time and with accuracy that is expected. That can be a lot of pressure to place on yourself, especially if you tend to be a person who agrees and gives into every demand. You may also think that you are really good at multitasking and can do various things at the same time, but the reality is that you cannot give one-hundred percent of your attention to the activity or task at hand if you are trying to do many things at once. You can easily feel overwhelmed by the many things that you need to do and find yourself rushing to get through everything feeling panicked and stressed.

Planning and prioritization can help you create some order to manage all the things that you need to do on any given day. Start by making a list of all the things that you need to get done on a particular day. Be realistic and cognizant of the fact that you only have so many hours in a day. Your ability to be able to get a number of tasks done on any particular day may be influenced by a variety of different factors.

Try not overestimate your ability and the available time you have to get something done. The reality is you will not be able to attend to all the emails in your inbox if you need to be on the road attending to errands for a few hours in the day, but may be able to work through half of your inbox. It can help to color code your list into work or business and personal activities so you can schedule these accordingly. Once you have your list, you need to decide how important each of the tasks is. You can categorize them as follows:

- Critical or High Priority: These are tasks and activities that are very important and need to be done today
- Moderate or Medium Priority: Tasks that could be done today, but are not critical and could be done at a later stage or the next day
- Minor or Low Priority: There will be things that are actually not important, and essentially it does not matter if it gets done today, next week or at all

It is very important that you are honest with yourself about how you prioritize each task. Believe it or not, not everything is absolutely critical, and there are some things that genuinely do not matter or will not add value in any way if you do not do them. Be realistic with your time and abilities. The hardest part is looking at your list and letting go of the minor tasks. Ultimately, you will feel more organized and in control which means, overall, less stressed about the things you need to accomplish in any given day. You can repeat this activity every morning, or the evening before if you will feel better knowing what lies ahead of you the following day. Overall, be kind yourself, don't take on more than you realistically have time to do and don't feel bad if something needs to be shelved or totally crossed off of the list.

Mindfulness and Meditation

Practicing meditation and mindfulness techniques can help you step away from a stressful situation and restore some calm and balance to your mind. It has proven to be effective in positively influencing your mood and gives you an increased ability to manage stressful situations. You can start practicing mindfulness and meditation techniques as part of the things that you do daily as part of your routine or use it as soon as you feel yourself becoming stressed and agitated in a particular situation. You can also refer to the Deep Breathing, Muscle Relaxation, Visualization and Counting techniques in the previous chapter which can also be useful in helping to manage your stress.

The goal of effective meditation is to bring your mind away from the outside distractions and stressors and into the present moment to create a sense of calm and well-being. As you go about your day, your mind is constantly racing with thoughts, and the thoughts that are causing you the most stress are those automatic negative thoughts that are constantly "on" in the back of your mind. Meditation and mindfulness is about creating your own bubble of a peaceful oasis inside your mind that you can escape to when feeling stressed and overwhelmed.

Find a quiet place free from distractions. It could be your bedroom, garden, deck, balcony or even an office or vacant meeting room. Sometimes even just sitting in your car before you get out and head to the office can provide the perfect place and time for meditation and mindfulness. Sit in a comfortable position, any position is fine as long as you are comfortable, and however you are sitting doesn't cause you any distractions or makes you feel uneasy.

Close your eyes and concentrate on your breathing, allowing all other thoughts to leave your mind. Become mindful of the air going into your nose and out of your mouth. Concentrate on the sensation of breathing in and out, your lungs filling with air and the movement of your diaphragm up and down. As you do this, other thoughts may enter your mind. You might wonder about something you need to do later in the day or that happened earlier, you might start daydreaming or recalling a past memory. That is ok, just become aware of the thought and move it out of your mind again, bringing your attention back to your breathing. Do this every time a thought enters your mind. It doesn't matter how many times it happens, just focus on pushing the thought away and bringing back focus to your breathing. Meditation practices become easier the more that you do them; it will be easier to focus on your breathing and the fewer thoughts will pop into your head.

You can start by trying to meditate for 10 minutes a day, then gradually increase to 15 minutes, then 20 minutes. The purpose of meditation is to find calm and be present, so it is important that you try and practice mindfulness every day, even if it is just for five minutes. The habit and routine of practicing meditation will soon become second nature as you see the benefits in lowering your levels of stress.

Realistic Probability

That little voice inside our head can very easily go off on a tangent and start creating all kinds of outcomes and situations that are often unrealistic and have a low likelihood of actually happening. Many of us have the habit of automatically thinking about the worst case scenario based on our automatic thoughts and beliefs. CBT is about recognizing your thoughts and beliefs, understanding why they are there and replacing them with realistic and positive thoughts. Much of our stress is caused by the automatic negative thinking as soon as we are dealing with a situation, person or activity that is causing us stress (*CBT Therapy for Stress, ABCT*, n.d.). The belief that things will always go either majorly wrong or go according to plan, leads to always thinking the worst will happen instead of looking at the situation realistically.

Next time you find yourself stressing over a particular situation, stop and think of the likelihood of outcomes. Will your boss actually fire you if the project you are working on doesn't work out as planned? Is there a realistic chance of missing your flight if you leave with enough time to get to the airport? Look at the probability of the outcome or different outcomes you have in your head. If there is only a very small chance of the worst case outcome actually happening, is it worth spending hours of your day or a sleepless night stressing about this highly unlikely outcome? Probably not.

Refocus your thoughts on the positive and realistic outcomes, instead of the negative and unlikely ones. If you are struggling to stop stressing and find calm, practice one of the techniques outlined above.

Thinking Differently

Cognitive Restructuring has been discussed in depth in the previous chapter and is a very effective tool in managing stress and stressful situations. You should implement this technique to help understand your thoughts and feelings to start developing positive thoughts instead. When you are feeling stressed by a particular situation or incident, try making a list of all of the emotions, thoughts and feelings you are having about the thing that is causing you stress. Using the Cognitive Restructuring technique, look at alternative feelings and thoughts to replace the negative ones you are experiencing.

You can also write down all of the emotions, thoughts and feelings on a piece of paper and then put it away until after that particular situation has passed. Then write down all of the actual emotions and feelings that happened when the situation really occurred. Take the two different pages and compare them. How many of the things you had thought would happen actually did? Were your feelings in the real-life situation different to what you had expected in your head? Now that you are able to see the reality of what happened, you can learn from that experience and adjust your thoughts and feelings for the future, knowing you have evidence to support the most probable outcome.

CHAPTER 5
MANAGING DEPRESSION

Depression affects millions of people all over the world and can affect anyone whether you are young or old, rich or poor, working or unemployed, have children or not, are married or live alone. Many of us will sometimes have a bad day caused by stress or a particular issue that is causing us emotional or physical discomfort. We feel a bit down, tired and generally a bit out of sorts, but it doesn't last for too long. Depression is when that feeling of despair does not go away, like a dark cloud that hangs heavy over your head. It starts to affect how you function on a daily basis and how you interact or avoid interaction with those around you. It can leave you feeling alienated and alone, just trying to function "normally" can seem like an impossible and overwhelming task. If left untreated, depression can have serious outcomes including reliance on alcohol and drugs and even suicidal thoughts. There is hope for those that suffer from depression, as it can be very treatable and there are many ways to help. From medication, to a variety of therapies, finding the treatment or combination of treatments that work for you will help make vast improvements in your everyday life and give you the confidence and skills to cope with the set-backs and challenges you may face in the future. While many sufferers of depression are able to manage with the help of medication, a combination of medication with CBT techniques has been shown to have a greater positive impact in treating depression, can have much longer lasting results and empower you with tools you can continue to use for years to come (Pathak, 2018).

CBT works by looking at the underlying thoughts and beliefs that lead to negative behaviors and impacts on moods and feelings. When you are feeling depressed or suffer from clinical depression, you will be well aware of how caught up you can get in your head and how strong the effects of those negative thoughts and beliefs are on your daily functioning. It is those thoughts and beliefs that fuel negativity and fear and lead you to feeling much worse about yourself and your circumstances, and impact your ability to function. By understanding and changing those negative thoughts and beliefs, you can work on changing them and learning how to replace them with new positive thinking that will help you manage your depression on a daily basis (Clancy, 2019).

Most people who suffer from depression have negative beliefs regarding themselves, the environment they are in and their feelings about the future. Negative beliefs can include thoughts like feeling worthless, believing the place where they live or work is terrible and believing that they will never get better or things will always be terrible. You may have fallen into a pattern of finding things to reinforce these negative beliefs by always looking for the negatives in any situation or event that occurs and ignoring the positive aspects, therefore reinforcing those feelings and beliefs to be true. You may be constantly overthinking everything that happens all the time, holding onto those negative feelings and beliefs and reliving them over and over again, never allowing yourself the chance to break-away from the situation, event or feeling and allowing the negativity to grow. Overgeneralizing is something else that you may be doing if you suffer from depression. Believing that if one bad thing happens, it means that something bad will always happen, or if a particular situation or event turned out badly that all future situations or events will also turn out badly. It's believing that because one bad thing happened to you in your life, that you feel or believe that your entire life is bad.

Signs and symptoms that you may be depressed include:

- Feeling hopeless and like you have the inability to help yourself feel better
- Not wanting to do the things that you used to enjoy
- Loss of change in appetite when nothing else in your life has changed, like starting a new diet or exercise plan
- General feeling of not being well or having unexplained aches and pains without any medical reason
- Reliance on alcohol or drugs "to get through the day"
- Constantly being tired all the time and wanting to sleep more than usual or at odd times of the day
- Unable to concentrate, even on simple and easy tasks
- Not liking yourself, feeling that you are worthless and general feelings of guilt

Changing Behaviors

If you find yourself feeling depressed, you may be more inclined to hide away and stay in bed, rather than trying to get involved in any social activities, household tasks, work or school and sometimes even neglecting basic hygiene. It seems a lot easier to avoid doing all of these things than trying to find the energy or desire to actually engage with people, places and activities. Unfortunately, this starts a cycle of negativity and by avoiding these things you end up feeling more depressed because you keep thinking about all the negative reasons why you can't do them, which means you feel less likely to do them in future and rationalize why you should keep avoiding them.

In order to break this cycle of negativity and avoidance, you can use the Cognitive Therapy technique of Pleasant Activity Scheduling to replace avoidance with activities that you enjoy or make you feel better about yourself, your environment or your future. By actively seeking to engage in pleasant activities, you will see how your mood improves after these activities, leaving you feeling better instead of worse and giving you increased motivation to continue to do things instead of actively avoiding them (Clancy, 2019). It's like positive mood reinforcement for your brain. The more things you do that make you feel happy or positive, the more likely you are to do things that make you feel happy or positive.

While the thought of doing anything at all may feel very overwhelming to start with, you don't have to jump in with a major activity like attending a big social gathering like a party, but instead start with smaller activities that are easier for you to do and gradually build up to the ones you really struggle with. Start by making a list of two different kinds of activities, ones that you find pleasurable and enjoy and ones that make you feel like you have achieved or accomplished something. Pleasurable activities can be things like going for a walk, reading a book, phoning a friend or playing with a pet. Accomplished activities are those that make you feel like you have achieved something, finishing a project for work or school, doing chores around the house or even simple things like making a phone call to schedule an appointment. Make sure that each of these lists have things that vary from easy and small, to harder and more complex. The idea is that you can start with the easier ones and work your way up to the harder ones.

Now that you have your lists of activities, look at your day ahead and make time to do one pleasurable activity and one accomplished activity. Depending on how you are feeling on that particular day, you could decide to do more than one or each, the important thing is that you start by doing something. It helps to have a diary or calendar, but you can write it down on a piece of paper. Try and plan as much of your day as possible, giving times for everything you need or have planned to do. This will leave you feeling much more in control of your day ahead and perhaps even a little proud that you managed to have a plan.

As you go through your day and complete your activities, rate each one on a scale of 1-10 for how much you felt the activity brought you pleasure or made you feel accomplished. Then give the activity an overall mood rating for how you felt while doing it. Over time, you will be able to identify which activities are the ones you felt the best doing and had the biggest feeling of pleasure or accomplishment and you can then use those for planning future activities. You will always want to do the things that worked out the most positively for you, so by keeping records, you have real-life evidence of how you actually felt instead of trying to imagine or thinking back to those activities with feelings of negativity because you are in a bad headspace on that particular day.

You might find yourself feeling a bit anxious as you make your list because you are unsure of how you will do a particular activity, how you might feel or how others may respond. It may help to do some roleplaying in your head or with a friend or your therapist. This kind of imaginary rehearsing can help you find any potential obstacles or challenges you may face doing that activity and start thinking about how you could solve them. Sometimes just having a plan for what we might expect to happen gives you the confidence to actually try and do the activity instead of avoiding it because of unknown factors. While working through this, you may also discover that some of the challenges or obstacles you think you might face are actually unrealistic or improbable which helps you to have a much more realistic view of what will actually happen instead of what you think might happen.

Changing Thoughts

In an earlier chapter, the CBT technique for Cognitive Restructuring and how to challenge and change your automatic thinking is discussed in depth with a step-by-step approach. When you are suffering from depression, these negative thoughts and beliefs are overwhelming and all-consuming and tend to be replayed over and over again leaving you feeling more depressed and negative. When using Cognitive Restructuring for depression, you may find you need to understand overarching thoughts and beliefs as well as smaller, more specific ones that could be related to your negative feelings and thoughts around a particular person, place or thing.

The goal of Cognitive Restructuring is to unpack those beliefs and thoughts by trying to find actual evidence which contradicts those negative beliefs in order to replace them with more positive thoughts (Cuncic, 2020). These thoughts and beliefs often become the underlying assumption that you use to decide how you will feel about something or you will use them to convince yourself to do or not to do something. Every negative thought you have influences your mood and behavior in some way, by replacing them with positive thoughts, you are already starting from a place of positivity rather than negativity and will be more likely to actually engage in activities and with others that will ultimately lead you to finding more positive reinforcement.

Individuals who suffer from depression often have thoughts that fall into the three different categories mentioned before: thoughts about oneself, thoughts about the environment and thoughts about the future. These negative thoughts can worsen symptoms of depression and feed into the cycle of negativity. Negative thoughts about yourself could include things like, "Nobody likes me" or, "I'm worthless," these are the things that you think about yourself and the type of person that you believe yourself to be. Negative thoughts about your environment are those about where you physically are, whether it is at home, school, work or even a particular place or event you need to go to. Thoughts about your environment could be things like, "I'm invisible at work," or, "My house will never be clean," or, "This country is going down the drain." Thoughts about your future that are negative could be things like, "Things will never get better," or, "I am going to mess up on this project," or, "My life will always be a failure." As you can see, having these negative thoughts always in your head will ultimately influence your mood and how you instinctively react to different situations you might find yourself in. If you constantly believe and think that you are worthless and will never succeed at work, you will find things that support those negative beliefs, which perpetuates the negative cycle.

Make a list of all the feelings that you have about yourself, your environment and your future. Then work your way down the list and ask yourself: What evidence do I have to support that belief? What evidence do I have to the contrary? Most people who suffer from depression will find that they have little actual concrete evidence to support their beliefs, but most often inaccurate assumptions they have created in their minds to support the negative belief they are holding onto. You need to be able to critically evaluate the evidence or assumptions you find, so it may be helpful to work with someone who has an unbiased view of the situation who can be an objective sounding board. Otherwise, you will only look for things that support your beliefs and thoughts and not actively engage in the Cognitive Restructuring technique.

Another great CBT technique to use on a regular basis is creating Thought Records, as discussed in Chapter 2. Thoughts Records focus on more situational based thoughts and beliefs, such as how you felt about a particular thing happening, rather than an overarching core belief about yourself. Thought Records are useful in developing alternative ways of thinking about particular things that happen as you need to actively look at all the reasons why a particular thing has or could have occurred and introduce a more positive way of thinking about the situation. Understanding that most of the time, the thoughts that you are thinking and the things you believe to be true, have actual evidence that doesn't support your negative view and ultimately leads to an inherently less depressed view of the situation and yourself. Remember that the thoughts and beliefs you have inside your head don't have to be true and there is always at least one other way to look at things, you just have to be open to finding those things and have the desire to try and change your thinking into a more positive space.

Will CBT Work?

As with anything in life, whether something works to help you or not depends entirely on you. You need to actually want to change and be open and willing to work on yourself and use the different techniques, either with a therapist or by yourself, in order for it to make any difference in your life. If you go into any kind of treatment for your depression already armed with the underlying negative thoughts, such as, I don't want to do this," and, "It's not going to work anyway," you have already set yourself up for failure.

Any kind of therapy, but especially CBT, will require you to be very honest with yourself and your thoughts. This can be hard and scary because it is difficult to face ourselves and our negative thoughts. It is perfectly normal that throughout this process you will feel uncomfortable and sometimes overwhelmed. Remember that you have spent a lot of time avoiding particular feelings and situations that you find depressing or distressing, so it is natural to find it difficult to deal with these things head-on.

You are in control of how much, how often and how deeply you engage with your thoughts, emotions and activities. So, you can move forward as quickly or slowly as you need and lower or increase the intensity as you progress. The tools and techniques that you learn through CBT will empower you with the skills to use in the future and will ultimately benefit you in the long-term.

CHAPTER 6
MANAGING FEARS AND PHOBIAS

Fears and phobias fall into the same grouping as anxiety disorders. While generalized anxiety disorder is usually wide ranging, covering a number of different kinds of situations or tasks that cause anxiety, fears and phobias are a lot more specific. Phobias are usually an extreme fear of a particular object, animal, place or activity that results in you experiencing symptoms of anxiety, including a physiological reaction (Jacobson, 2011). This feeling of anxiety may be present, even if the object of the fear or phobia isn't able to cause you any harm. For example, having a phobia with spiders and feeling anxious when you see a picture of one on the television, even when you know that the spider on the television can't harm you in any way. Fears and phobias can sometimes be irrational, while other times may be based on a past experience. Many people will be able to function quite normally while having a particular fear and phobia and they may not require any form of treatment, however, if your fear or phobia is having an impact in your everyday life or preventing you from doing something that you really enjoy or if the fear itself is much bigger than the actual danger it presents, you may want to consider seeking treatment.

Phobias generally don't just start from nowhere and can originate from either a past traumatic experience or it could be a fear or phobia you inherited from a parent or caregiver. Phobias can even develop as part of ongoing or repeated negative exposure. If you fell into a swimming pool when you were much younger, you may have developed a fear of drowning as a result. This fear may have meant that you never learnt to swim and as a result you now find that you are missing out on many social activities or feel that you will have too much anxiety to go on a holiday cruise. Sometimes, a parent or caregiver may have a fear or phobia and although you may not have even had a negative experience regarding that particular object, animal or situation, you also develop that same fear. If your mother had a fear of heights and every time you went up stairs or stood on a balcony she would get anxious and fearful, by exposing you to her anxiety around her particular phobia you may develop the same fear or phobia. Repeated negative exposure to an object, animal or situation can also lead you to develop a fear or phobia. If every day on your way to school you passed a dog who looked scary and barked at you, you could easily develop a fear of dogs due to the repeated negative exposure and experience you had.

CBT is supported in being very effective for treating anxiety and more specific fears and phobias through Situation Exposure, Cognitive Restructuring and practicing Mindfulness and Meditation (Fritscher, 2008). Your fear and phobia is driven by a particular set of thoughts and beliefs that cause an overreaction to that particular object, animal or situation. These techniques challenge those thoughts and beliefs and systematically train you to handle your fears and phobias better.

Types of Phobias

Phobias fall into one of two different categories, specific or complex phobias (Mind for Better Health, 2017). Specific phobias are specific objects, animals or situations; while complex phobias have a greater impact on your everyday life and often develop in early adulthood. Complex phobias are things like a fear of people or social situations that cause excessive anxiety or agoraphobia, which is the fear of being in places which may cause embarrassment or being unable to leave.

Specific Phobias

The common type of phobias are specific phobias. Almost everyone has had something that they have been scared of. Most specific phobias start very early on in childhood and can either get better or worse as you get older. Examples of specific phobias include:

- Animals like spiders, snakes, cats, dogs, rats or other insects
- Situations like being in the dark, a fear of flying, small spaces, being scared of going to the doctor
- Phobias about the natural environment like being scared of heights, fear of open water, being afraid of storms or lightning
- Body-based phobias relates to fears about seeing blood, vomiting, giving birth, needles or choking
- There things that fall outside of these specific categories like being scared of certain foods or people dressed up in characters, like clowns

There are many things that people can develop fears and phobias about, and this list is not exhaustive. Your fear or phobia could be about almost anything and if it is causing you to have feelings of anxiety even when there is no danger present and it is having an impact on your everyday life, CBT techniques can help you manage that fear.

Complex Phobias

Complex phobias are also called social phobias or agoraphobias. They can have a much bigger negative impact on your daily functioning as they include social situations of which many may be unavoidable in your daily life and make it difficult to function.

- Social phobias include activities like public speaking, meeting new people, talking on the telephone, and even going to work or doing regular activities like shopping
- Agoraphobia is the fear of particular situations or places, like crowded malls, travelling on a bus or a train or in car, or being in closed spaces

Many people develop complex phobias after experiencing a panic attack after being in a particular social situation or specific place. The fear of having another panic attack if you are in the same situation or place again can cause you to feel heightened levels of anxiety and develop a specific complex phobia following that incident. All human beings have the natural instinct to avoid situations which cause us distress, so it is not uncommon to develop fears and phobias in response to stressful situations that have caused intense anxiety in the past.

Gradual Exposure

Exposing yourself gradually to your particular fear and phobia through Situation Exposure technique is a part of CBT. Chapter 3 gives a very thorough explanation of this technique and how it can be used to manage anxiety and situations which cause anxiety. It also provides specific tools including deep breathing techniques, visualization, muscle relaxation and counting techniques to help immediately manage rising levels of anxiety and calm yourself down.

By gradual, planned exposure to your particular fear or phobia you can start to develop a tolerance and learn how to effectively manage your anxiety around your particular phobia by starting out with small levels of exposure and building up to more intensity (*Phobia Treatment*, n.d.). Start by having a goal in mind of what you want to achieve. If you have a fear of dogs, but really want to go to visit a friend who has several dogs at their house, you can have visiting that friend as your ultimate goal. If you have a fear of flying, you could have flying to a special destination holiday as the goal you are working towards. It doesn't have to be overly ambitious, depending on the level of anxiety you have regarding your particular fear, working toward a big goal might cause you even more distress, so try and find an intermediate goal that you feel comfortable working toward, and then you can tackle the harder one when you feel confident enough to do so.

The next step is to make a list of between 10 to 20 different steps or activities to gradually increase exposure and work toward your goal (Jacobson, 2011). If you have a fear of snakes, you might start with looking at pictures of snakes, then watching a video of a snake. The next step might be to look at a harmless snake in real life, but from a safe distance, and following that, looking at a more dangerous snake in real life from a safe distance. Only once you feel comfortable doing one particular step, will you move onto the next one. You shouldn't jump straight into holding a harmless snake, if you haven't managed to control your anxiety just looking at a harmless snake from a safe distance. There is no set timeline or deadline for completing a step, so you can take as long as you need before moving on. If you feel like perhaps you've moved a bit too quickly, you can always go back one or two steps and work through your anxiety with those again.

When you are exposed to your fear or phobia, you will immediately have a physical or emotional response to that fear. You need to learn how to manage those responses and calm your anxiety so you face your fear. Deep breathing techniques are very helpful in situational exposure therapy.

Retrain Your Brain

Cognitive Restructuring is a core technique in using CBT to treat a variety of disorders. Fears and phobias are irrational fears that trigger heightened responses and impact your daily functioning. Using Cognitive Restructuring you can start to understand where the fear comes from, identify the automatic thoughts and triggers that cause the emotional response and develop new and positive thinking to help you overcome your fear or phobia.

Identify the underlying thoughts and feelings you have when you are exposed to your particular fear or phobia. If you have a fear of flying, whenever you see an airplane you might be filled with anxiety that the plan is going to crash. Why do you have this thought and feeling? Is it rational or irrational? Have you or someone you know ever been in a plane crash or seen a plane crash that triggered this fear? Understanding where the fear or phobia comes from can help you identify why you might have those thoughts and feelings.

The next step is to start to question whether the thoughts and feelings you have about your fear are based on facts or emotions. Do you have evidence to support your thoughts or evidence that proves your thoughts and feelings about your fear is in fact incorrect? You can also ask yourself what is the worst possible outcome that could happen if this actually happens? What will you do in that situation? Are there alternative or different outcomes or realistic thoughts and feelings that could also happen in this situation? By questioning what you believe to be true, you can start to look at the fear or phobia from a different perspective. For example, you may believe that all dogs will bite you, but by looking at all the evidence and possible alternative outcomes, you might come to the conclusion that not all dogs bite and realistically, a dog that is known to you or is very well trained has a very unlikely chance of biting you. Now, the next time that you see a dog or come into contact with a dog, instead of immediately allowing the automatic "worst case scenario" thoughts and feelings to overwhelm you, you start to replace those thoughts with the new, more realistic and balanced, evidence-based thinking you have worked on.

Staying Calm

When dealing with fears and phobias, you can sometimes find yourself in a situation where you may be unintentionally exposed to your phobia or get caught unaware by your rising levels of anxiety and have a panic attack. You can learn tools and techniques that can help you manage your levels of panic and anxiety in that particular situation and help you stay calm so you can handle the situation better or become able to calmly remove yourself from the situation that is causing you discomfort. It can be easier to learn to cope with the feelings of fear, anxiety or panic than it may be to try and avoid feeling that way.

Take a Deep Breath

One of the most effective techniques to calming yourself down in the midst of a fear or phobia induced panic attack is to practice deep breathing. By regaining control over your breathing, you can avoid hyperventilating that could add to your feelings of distress (Ankrom, 2019). Focus on your breathing and close your eyes. Take a deep breath into your nose while counting to four, then hold for two seconds, then breath out for four counts. Repeat this breathing pattern and focus on your breathing and the counting until you feel your heart rate lowering a sense of calm returning.

It's Only Temporary

Sometimes the most powerful tool you have is to remind yourself, and your brain, that the current situation, fear or phobia that you are exposed to is only temporary. You will not be in this situation forever, you will be ok and this will pass. If you are afraid of a lightning storm, your logical brain knows that the storm will eventually pass and it can help to remind yourself of that fact instead of allowing the physical emotions and responses to become overwhelming.

It can help to have a reassuring mantra that you use and can say to yourself over and over again. By repeating your mantra you are able to start shifting your mental focus away from the anxiety and on the repetition of the mantra. Find a particular phrase that makes you feel calm and in control. It can also help to reinforce the positive thinking you are working on when retraining your brain through Cognitive Restructuring. Some examples could be saying, "I am not in any danger," or, "This too shall pass," and, "I am safe. I am calm."

Take Your Mind Away From the Fear

Practicing mindfulness can help to keep you distracted from the distressing situation caused by your fear or phobia and help ground you in the reality of the situation and not get pulled into the fear caused by your rising anxiety. For example, if you see a rat run across your path and you have a fear of rodents, it helps to bring your mind to where you physically are. Concentrate on where you are standing, take a moment to feel the air on your face, remove your thoughts from the rat and instead focus on your physical presence and sensations that you know and are comfortable with.

You can also use some of the Mindfulness and Meditation techniques discussed in Chapter 4.

Another way to take your mind off of the feelings of fear and anxiety is to find something else to focus on. Pick an object that you can easily see in close proximity, and shift all of your focus onto that object. What does it look like? How big is it? What color is it? What do you think it feels like? Use all your energy to really focus on this object and away from the anxiety caused by your fear or phobia.

Medication and Natural Remedies

If your fear or phobia is so severe that it causes debilitating panic attacks, speak to your doctor about specific medications that may help and that you can keep with you in case of emergency.

Many natural remedies and essential oils have a calming and relaxing effect. Lavender and chamomile are known for having calming properties and can help you relax in distressing situations. Put some of the essential oil on your wrists and inhale the scent deeply. Combine this with deep breathing techniques for maximum effects.

Speak to your doctor if you plan on using any natural remedies or essential oils, as if you are already on certain kinds of medications, it could have an adverse reaction. Always seek professional medical help when using any kind of medication, whether it is over-the-counter or prescription, and even natural or homeopathic remedies.

CHAPTER 7
MANAGING ADDICTION

Addiction is a very complex and complicated disorder. It is a compulsive disorder, where the person engages in ongoing behaviors that they have no control over. Even though the addict may want to stop or change their behavior, they are unable to do so. They engage in compulsive behavior because they develop a physical dependence on their addiction that is driven by beliefs, thoughts and feelings making them believe that they need their addiction in order to survive. Addiction can have far reaching consequences for both the person who is addicted and those around them, as this mental obsession and physical dependence can lead them to engage in reckless and hurtful behaviors.

The behavior and addiction itself is progressive and often starts out in a mild form, slowly increasing in frequency and intensity, until the addict has little or no control over their addiction and the compulsive behaviors they are engaging in. This can be detrimental, as without proper treatment, many addicts deteriorate to such an extent that they might die or become institutionalized. Unfortunately, many addicts will believe that they do not have a problem and that they have everything under control. This may cause them to push away friends and family who want to try and help them. Only when an addict is prepared to accept that they have a problem and has a desire and willingness to make changes and start to recover, will they be able to accept help.

CBT aims to help the addict understand and identify the thoughts, circumstances and issues that are related to or causing their addiction. By understanding the negative thoughts that are contributing to the addiction, you can start to replace them with positive thoughts, feelings and behaviors which will positively impact your recovery.

Types of Addiction

There are many people that overindulge in drinking or eating or have specific things that they do on a regular basis like gambling, sex or even exercise. Just because you or someone you know does something a lot or repeatedly, does not necessarily mean that they have an addiction. Having an addiction means having a mental or physical obsession that causes harm to yourself or those around you. If you are overindulging in anything that is causing problems with your relationships, making you feel bad about yourself, or is having negative consequences in your life, you may have a problem. Addiction can take many forms, and doesn't necessarily need to be a substance, but could also be an activity or any kind of other compulsive behavior (Addiction Helper, 2012).

Substance Addiction

A substance addiction is probably the one you are most familiar with, as when you think of addiction you probably think about drugs or alcohol However, you could develop an addiction to almost any substance. Some of the most common substances that people become addicted to are:

- alcohol
- cannabis
- nicotine
- methamphetamines
- prescription drugs
- opioids
- sugar
- caffeine

Some substances have chemically addictive properties, making it even more difficult to stop using them. When the physical dependency is so great, often medical intervention is required in addition to psychological treatment to help with overcoming the addiction.

Behavioral Addictions

Behavioral addictions are those that result in the compulsive engagement in particular behaviors. These behaviors or activities done on their own or on a regular basis could in fact be normal, healthy behaviors, but if they start to affect how the person is living their life and having negative consequences for themselves or those around them, it can signal a problem and the possibility that they may be engaging in addictive behaviors.

- gambling
- sex
- exercise
- shopping
- social media or phone usage
- pornography
- video games
- over eating

This list is not exhaustive, and any activity that becomes something that you do compulsively and is causing problems is your life could be a sign of an addiction.

Finding Thought Patterns

CBT looks at finding the connection between your underlying thoughts and how they impact your feelings, emotions and ultimately your behavior and actions. With addiction, it is those underlying thoughts that can be very damaging and often stand in the way of the addict getting help or having a successful recovery (Addiction Helper, 2012). If an addict can be helped to understand the underlying thoughts that are driving their compulsive behaviors, they will be in a position to make positive changes and hopefully overcome their addictive patterns.

Often the automatic thoughts you have make you feel uncomfortable, angry or sad. Depression, anxiety and other similar disorders are often quite prevalent with those who suffer from some kind of addiction. Addicts use substances or behaviors to try and numb the feelings of negativity they are experiencing or to use the substances and activities to try and escape from the "real world" so they do not have to deal with how they are feeling or how those thoughts and feelings are affecting their lives.

Using CBT techniques, addicts can help to identify their automatic thoughts and the irrational or false thoughts and beliefs that lead them to seek relief in addictive substances or behaviors. Understanding what these thoughts are, they can find thought patterns that are triggering to their addiction and learn to manage these triggers (Polansky, 2019). Developing coping skills to deal with addiction and life in recovery is an essential tool to make sure that you will be equipped in the best possible way to deal with life on life's terms. The reality is that once you remove the addictive substance or behavior, your old thoughts are still there and life around you will carry on as normal. If the underlying problems are not addressed and you are not equipped with skills to deal with the challenges you will face, there is a strong chance that you fall back into old behaviors and thoughts, and eventually return to your addiction.

Thought Records are a powerful tool for use in treating addiction with CBT. This technique is discussed in detail in previous chapters and is used in much the same way for treating addiction. Making a list of all the automatic thoughts and beliefs you have will help you understand what is influencing your addictive behaviors. Most of the things we hold to be true, are unrealistic, untrue and can even be impossible standards that we attempt to hold ourselves to. Thought records are there to help you interrogate those underlying thoughts and use evidence to help show you that those thoughts can be challenged and changed. These negative thought patterns are often linked to certain triggers that cause us to respond with negative behaviors or turn to the addition to cope. If you can identify the triggers associated with those thought patterns, you can learn to avoid them and implement positive techniques to deal with them instead of the negative reliance on the addiction or compulsive behaviors.

Understanding the Impact of Behavior

Addicts often don't think that what they are doing is causing any harm, other than to themselves, until they are already deep into the addiction. They continuously engage in compulsive and destructive behaviors because they genuinely believe that there is no other way. Behavioral experiments can be a powerful technique to help you understand the impact of your negative behavior in contrast to the alternative positive behavior. Using Behavioral Experiments, you can start exchanging negative thoughts for positive thoughts and see how they impact changes in your behavior. For example, a binge drinker is always consumed with feelings of immense guilt after a binge episode. The person then berates themselves for their behavior, believing that if they are harsh, they will "kick themselves into gear" and not engage in this same behavior in future because they feel bad about it and themselves. This just perpetuates a cycle of negativity. Instead, they can choose to replace the negative response with a positive one by being kinder to themselves, understanding that it is ok to make a mistake, as long as they learn from it. Use the negative behavior to help identify the trigger and negative thoughts that resulted in the behavior so you are equipped to handle it better if it happens again. You will be surprised by the power of positivity and how that influences our ongoing choices and behaviors. By constantly challenging negative thoughts and behaviors with positive ones, positivity will slowly start to take the place of negative thinking.

Before an addict even picks up that drink, drug or decides to engage in that compulsive behavior, they have already begun thinking about what it is they are going to do. Using Behavioral Experiments, addicts can use past behaviors and the outcomes to understand what happened and identify patterns or triggers to avoid it happening again. They can also use Behavioral Experiments to "play the story to the end" as a good indication of what a future outcome might be and what a past outcome was. For example, if every time in the past you have gone out with a certain person or spent more than a certain amount of time gambling, there has always been a negative consequence, you can use that information to understand that if you do the exact same thing the outcome will almost definitely be a negative one. Being able to look at an upcoming situation or understand a particular thought or feeling you are currently having against evidence of what has happened in the past, can help you make better choices in the future. The same applies for all past behaviors or new behaviors that have had a positive outcome. For example, "Every time I talk with Sam, she always makes me feel better and talks me out of bad decisions." The next time you are feeling sad or in a bad space, you can refer back to how you dealt with the situation and the fact that it had a positive outcome, to reinforce positive patterns in behavior. We are always more likely to carry on doing something if it makes us feel better or if it has a positive outcome, than if there are negative consequences or it makes us feel bad.

Imagery Exposure

Often we find particular memories, images or past experiences cause negative feelings and can result in negative behaviors. Just like Situational Exposure is an effective technique to deal with anxiety, fears and phobias, Imagery Exposure can be used to desensitize an addict to triggers and memories that have led them to seek relief in substances and negative compulsive behaviors (Polansky, 2019).

Revisit and imagine a particular person, place or memory in your mind, that has caused you to feel pain, anxiety or discomfort. Most often these things are the triggers that lead you to feel negatively. Imagine every detail of the situation. Think about the smells, sounds and the feelings that you felt. If you start to feel overwhelmed, use a calming technique to bring you back to the present and away from the trigger.

Once you have a clear picture in your mind and you understand the feelings that you are feeling, start to imagine how you would handle the situation differently to achieve a positive outcome. This imaginary role play can help you develop self-confidence and problem solving skills to enable you to handle the situation or trigger when you encounter it in real life. For example, you imagine that you are driving near the turn-off to the liquor store that you always stop at. You feel anxious because the last time you stopped at the liquor store you got very drunk that evening and had a huge fight with your partner. You imagine yourself breathing deeply and counting slowly until you drive past the turn off and away from the liquor store. You now feel at ease and calm. This will help you the next time you are in the real life situation, as you can implement the actions and techniques you did in your imaginary "run-through" and feel more confident and self-assured that you will be able to handle the trigger or situation and there will be a positive outcome.

Plan to Do Things You Enjoy

Often the life of an addict is consumed with the compulsion of the negative behaviors and engaging in the addiction. This means that many of the things that you used to do, you are no longer doing and instead are focusing only on doing things as part of your addictive behavior.

Pleasant Activity Scheduling, an effective CBT tool, used in treating depression and other disorders, can help you get back into a "normal" routine again and find other activities that you can do that will bring you just as much enjoyment, in a healthier, more productive way than the addictive and compulsive behavior did (Hartney, 2020).

By planning your day or week ahead and including doing things that you enjoy, means that you will feel better about yourself, reduce negative thoughts and feelings and be less inclined to engage in undesirable behaviors. Making a list of all the healthy and positive things you enjoy doing or wish you had the time to do, but were always "too busy" is a good place to start. Now look at your schedule and start slotting in those activities throughout your day and week, so you have planned out what you are going to do. Having a plan makes you less likely to feel bored and go out looking to engage in destructive behaviors. Also try to schedule enjoyable and positive activities over times that you know are triggers or when you used to do compulsive things. For example, if you always went to the bar after work to have a drink, or five, instead schedule a walk with a friend for that same time. Often by including others in your planned activities, it can help hold you accountable for making sure that you do it, instead of making excuses to slip back into old patterns of behaviors.

Find Your "Happy Place"

Meditation and mindfulness techniques are excellent tools for helping you find calm within the chaos. It is very common for an addict to get caught up in their own heads, which can lead to feelings of anxiety and feeling overwhelmed. By starting with just five minutes a day of mindfulness and meditation, you can start to introduce feelings of calm and feel better prepared to tackle difficult situations. By emptying your mind of stressful situations, you will start to improve your mental health and well-being and develop resilience to handle stressful situations. Chapter 4 details techniques that you can use to start practicing mindfulness and meditation.

Often the actions and compulsive behaviors of addicts are impulsive, which is why being able to learn techniques to help you focus on being in the present moment in order to find calm and clarity, can help you to restore balance in your thinking and behaviors.

Additional Support

Addiction is a very hard thing to overcome and depending on the severity and length of the addiction, it may be a good idea to use Cognitive Behavioral Techniques together with other specialized forms of treatment and therapy. If you find that you are repeatedly falling back into old habits of negative thinking and compulsive behaviors, it is a good idea to reach out to someone who can assist you with additional support. Many addicts have had great success using Cognitive Behavioral Techniques in combination with Twelve Step Programs, group therapy, rehabilitation centers and professional psychological support.

Don't be afraid to seek help if you know that you are unable to control your addiction on your own. Leaving your addiction to progressively deteriorate can have permanent and irreversible impacts on your health, emotional wellbeing, relationships and financial circumstances. It is not a sign of weakness to seek assistance or help. It is a very difficult thing to be able to identify that you need help, and being able to step-up and reach for help is a sign of strength, self-worth and resilience. With the right kind of assistance and help, you will be able to overcome your addiction and start to rebuild your life in a positive way.

CHAPTER 8
SUPPORT AND GUIDANCE

When undergoing any kind of therapy, having support and guidance can really help you stay on track and get the most out of the therapy you are undertaking. While CBT is a fairly easy therapy to work on by yourself due to the fact that the various different techniques are quite structured and enable you to work through them step-by-step, it can sometimes feel quite overwhelming when you are working them on your own. It can be easy to feel unmotivated if you aren't seeing the kind of progress that you expect from yourself. Having realistic expectations and setting yourself small, but achievable and measurable goals can help to keep you focused on each goal and you will find yourself motivated to move onto the next goal as you accomplish each milestone. Striving for continuous progress rather than trying to reach your end goal all at once, will enable you to keep moving forward.

Different Kind of Support Structures

You are not alone. You are surrounded by many people who want to help you succeed and achieve your goals. Already by deciding to seek help through using CBT is a positive step in the right direction. Support structures are important because everyone needs someone, whether it is an individual, a group or a professional, that you can talk to when you need to. Sometimes you may need someone to just be able to say a few kind words or, if you are having a particularly difficult day or if you are going through a very unsettling situation, being able to turn to your support structure will help guide and advise you on how to deal with the issue and move forward. Your support structure doesn't necessarily need to help you specifically with working through CBT techniques, although that will be very useful, it could just be someone or a group of people that help keep you grounded and focused on everyday life and the normal daily challenges you face (Cherry, 2018). Most of the time, we just want to feel that we are not alone and that we know we can turn to someone who cares. Just feeling better about yourself can help keep you motivated to work on your therapy.

Everyone is different, and not everyone responds or needs the same kind of support. You might be a very private and personal person who would rather have a smaller or more individual support structure to help you focus on working through the specific CBT techniques. Many people also respond better to working with other people who are experiencing the same difficulties and who can relate to what you are going through. The important thing is that you have the right kind of support structures that work for you and provide you with the right kind of support that you need at any given time. Besides the different kinds of support structures that you may need, it is also important to understand and identify the correct kind of support that you may need to help you as you use CBT to deal with your specific disorder or challenges.

Emotional Support

Emotional support is the kind of support you need when you are going through tough or stressful times. Being able to unload emotions and have someone listen with care and empathy can help you feel better and more equipped to handle situations that may be emotionally distressing. While working through the various CBT techniques, life carries on and sometimes it can mean something happens outside of the disorder you are dealing with through the therapy. It will help to be able to turn to your support structure for emotional support in order for it not to take the focus away from your therapy and keep you on track in other aspects of your life.

Instrumental Support

You may not always be able to take care of all your physical needs, especially when you are going through many different emotions or your particular disorder is debilitating and interfering with you being able to manage on a daily basis. Sometimes you can be so focused on your emotional needs that you are unable to physically take care of yourself. Being able to have a support structure that can help you with your physical needs, will mean you have fewer things to worry about and one less distraction taking your focus away from using CBT. It could be as simple as having someone who is able to give you a lift to work or school or making sure that you have groceries in your fridge. If you spend so much time worrying about how you will get to work every day, it will take up a lot of your emotional energy and you may find yourself making excuses not to work on your particular disorder because you are too concerned with the physical needs that need to be met. Don't be scared to reach out to your support structure and tell them what you need assistance with. It may even help to explain why you need assistance with those things, so they know that by helping with your physical needs they are, in fact, helping you stay focused on your CBT.

Informational Support

Having access to the correct kind of information that can help you make decisions, manage difficult situations or provide you with guidance can help give you confidence to work through challenging or difficult situations. You may be faced with a decision which you might feel uncertain about, being able to reach out for informational support can help give you confidence in dealing with it, if you are able to get correct and helpful information. If there are certain aspects of your life, or a specific situation that comes up and you feel like you are lacking information to work through it, you may feel stuck and unable to move forward. Finding a support structure that can give you the correct and helpful information will empower you to make better choices. While working through the different CBT techniques, you might find that you need more in-depth information, support, or guidance to help you understand a specific technique better. There are many online resources, knowledgeable individuals, professionals and even friends or family that can help give you informational support in order to keep you working toward your goals.

Staying on Track With CBT

As with starting any kind of therapy, staying motivated and keeping with it can be very difficult. When you start anything new, you begin with the hope that it will be successful, but as you progress, it is easy to become distracted and unmotivated, especially if you have high expectations that may be taking a little longer than you had hoped to meet. CBT is not a once off cure all. It is a progressive therapy that takes time to work through the techniques to achieve what you need.

The first step is to understand why it is that you have decided to use CBT. Try to be clear about the real, tangible reason behind your decision. If you can understand the purpose behind why it is that you have decided to start, it can help keep you focused on keeping your intention where it needs to be.

Have a clear goal in mind of what you want to accomplish. CBT, in itself, requires you to have a goal in mind for what outcome it is that you are working toward. Make sure that your end goal is something that you can do. Be clear, concise and consistent. Don't shift your goal post and keep your ultimate goal in mind as you work through the different techniques. If you are easily caught up in the obstacles or feel like it is just getting too hard to stick with, it will help to remind yourself of where you are headed and what you are working toward (Daskal, 2016).

Make a plan with a clear vision that you believe in. Don't do this for anyone other than yourself. Look ahead and see yourself achieving your goal. It can help to break your end goal down into smaller "bite-size" chunks. It will be easier to stay motivated if you can see incremental achievements along the way. As you achieve each smaller goal, you will be motivated to keep going. You should also make sure that you schedule and set aside specific time to work on your therapy. This will help you keep focused to stay on track and ensure you make consistent progress. It is easy to get distracted or to feel like you are too busy when you don't have a schedule to work with.

Stay positive! You can do this! Having a positive mindset will result in positive actions. If you know that you generally find it very difficult to stay positive, try to find positive sayings, quotes and affirmations that you can use every day or before you start working on a specific technique. Never underestimate the power of positive thinking to keep you motivated and in the right headspace. Write down all your positive phrases and stick them up somewhere where you can see them every day so you are constantly being reminded of staying positive and are reinforcing those thoughts.

It can be difficult to stay motivated and stick with your goals if you are unorganized and working in a cluttered space. To assist you in making sure that you maintain your focus while working through the CBT techniques, consider creating a separate workspace in your home that you can use specifically for this purpose. Rather than using many pieces of paper or loose worksheets, having a notebook and a notice board that you use just for your therapy can help keep you focused and minimize distractions. It will also make keeping track of your progress easier and you will waste less time trying to get organized and start on your techniques every day.

Visualization is a powerful CBT technique and you can use it to stay motivated and ensure that you keep focused on what you are working toward. You have already decided to try CBT to work on a particular disorder. You have an end goal and clearly understand what you are trying to achieve. You also have a step-by-step plan on how you plan on achieving that goal. Now, visualize yourself achieving that goal. Imagine how you will feel and what it will look like to achieve success. If your goal is being able to go to that party, imagine yourself at that party, surrounded by friends and feeling happy, calm and secure. You might be using CBT to work on your fear of public speaking; imagine yourself standing up in the boardroom giving your presentation being well prepared, professional and concise in your delivery. The words come easily and clearly and you feel confident and in control. Imagine yourself at the end of each goal, doing exactly what you set out to do with the help of Cognitive Therapy techniques.

When to Seek Professional Help

Many individuals decide to take the "self-help" route to try and solve the problems, challenges or disorders that they are struggling with. You may be afraid to seek professional help because you don't think that your issue is that severe or you may have had a bad previous experience with a therapist or counsellor. There are many reasons that people choose to use CBT techniques on their own, instead of with a professional. That is perfectly ok and you may find that it works for you to be able to work on your particular issue on your own, with just the help of your immediate support systems. However, you may find you would rather use these techniques while working with a medical professional because it feels too overwhelming to do on your own, or because your condition is so severe that you will benefit more from working with someone medically and psychologically trained to work with CBT techniques.

Be honest with yourself about what it is that you are trying to work on; is it a small problem that is having an impact on your life or you feel is holding you back, or is it more complex and debilitating? If your condition is so severe that you cannot function on a daily basis or is having a significantly negative impact on all areas of your life, you may want to use CBT in combination with support from a medical professional. The techniques discussed in this book refer to specific areas or disorders with a fairly narrow and broad focus, but if the problems you are facing are very specific and you need a more nuanced approach to therapy, you may benefit from professional assistance.

If you are unsure whether you can use CBT on your own or if you need to work with a professional, it can help just to start on your own and see how you progress. Set yourself milestones where you can honestly evaluate your progress and objectively look at how you are progressing. If you find yourself really struggling with a particular step or technique and are not making any progress, it could be worthwhile talking to someone about why that may be the case as you may be overlooking a more complex issue.

CBT relies on the fact that you need to be completely honest about your negative thoughts, feelings and beliefs. If you cannot be honest with and about yourself, CBT will not work for you. It can be very difficult to be honest about why we think the way we do, what we think deep down about ourselves, and even finding alternative thoughts to challenge those negative thoughts, beliefs and feelings. Sometimes finding someone who can offer objective advice and support may be the only option to ensure that you deal with your disorder effectively and see authentic results.

Working on yourself is very hard. It takes time and dedication to see real positive improvement. If you find yourself easily distracted or you keep making excuses to avoid working on yourself, you may need someone who can help keep you on track. Knowing that you have a therapist or counsellor who you are accountable to and will keep you motivated may be the better option to work through CBT techniques with. You need to be consistent with your therapy, whether on your own or working with a professional, in order to see positive change. Having someone to work with who can look holistically at your particular situation and understand what your challenges are can have a major benefit in finding a way forward that will work for you.

Whether you decide to use CBT on your own, with a therapist or with the help of a support group, it has been proven to be successful in overcoming many different disorders and challenges. Seeking help is the first step you can make to seeing positive change and overcoming negative thoughts and behaviors in your everyday life. There is no failure in seeking professional medical help and can only benefit you in the long-term. It may even help you to work through issues, behaviors and disorders that you may not have even been aware of to begin with.

CONCLUSION

The most amazing thing about your brain is that it can constantly learn, adapt and thrive. The power to change your thoughts, beliefs and feelings that result in your behavior and actions from a negative space to a positive space is within your control. CBT offers you the opportunity to start making those changes through the various techniques, enabling you to tackle the negativity head on and gradually replace it with positivity. Research from medical professionals has proven that CBT is one of the most effective therapies used for treating many different psychological and emotional disorders. The skills and tools you learn through CBT techniques will continue to provide value and help you well after you finish working through whichever disorder, problem or challenge you have decided to work through and resolve.

Whether you are dealing with a psychological or emotional disorder, are struggling to cope with everyday life, or are just trying to shift your thinking, CBT techniques will help you in being able to understand and identify negative thought patterns and ways of thinking and help move you into a more positive mindset.

Cycles of negativity are driven by feelings of self-doubt and only ever being able to see the negative and never the positive. This can have a detrimental effect in all areas of your life, not only affecting how you see yourself and the world around you, but also influence your behavior and interactions or avoidance of others. CBT can offer you a solution to help break that cycle of negativity and start living your life the best way that you can. By deciding to read this book, you have already started to acknowledge that you need some kind of help with the disorder, problem or challenge you are facing in your life, which is a positive step in the right direction. It can be very difficult to really look at yourself, your thinking and your behavior and realize that there is a problem. Sometimes it is easier to live in denial instead of facing our issues rather than decide to make positive changes. It may take a significant push from a loved one or particularly impactful incident to make us realize that we do need to get some kind of help.

CBT, through its various different techniques and tools, offers you many different ways of starting to work on your negative thinking and making positive changes in your life. Whether you are working through these tools and techniques on your own, with support from friends or family or with a medical professional, you will start to see positive changes taking place which will give you the motivation to continue and find relief and success. Sometimes just starting with a small thing you want to change can be the catalyst in driving you toward bigger, more impactful changes you want to make. The tools and techniques CBT teaches you are simple, yet effective, and the only obstacle that you may face is your own ability to learn how to put them into practice.

Just like learning anything new, the key to making progress is having the commitment to stick with it. Retraining your brain from thinking negatively to thinking positively through CBT techniques requires you to put what you learn into action every single day. While it can be hard to start with, by getting into the habit of using the tools and skills you have learnt on a daily basis you will start to see positive progress and growth in how your thoughts, feelings and behaviors start to change. With practice, you will start to develop resilience in handling stressful and uncomfortable situations through using these tools and techniques and your brain will start shifting from always looking at the negative "worse-case-scenario" to being able to recognize the thoughts and shift your mindset into a more positive one.

While CBT may not work for everyone or every single different kind of emotional or psychological disorder, you can start by doing a few things in order to get the most out of working through, learning and implementing the tools and techniques you want to use.

Work together in partnership with your therapist or support structure. You will find that CBT will give you the best results if you work together with someone to help you identify what the core issues are that you need to work on and put together clearly defined goals you can work toward. This is not a "you versus them" situation. Understanding that anyone who is assisting you only wants the best for you and wants you to succeed will help you better work through the therapy.

Honesty and openness is the cornerstone of all CBT techniques. You need to be honest with yourself at all times to help you identify the negative thoughts and beliefs that are driving your negative ways of thinking. If you only recognize half of your negative thoughts and underlying beliefs and assumptions, you will only be able to deal with half of the things you want to change. Be honest with the people who you are working with and who are supporting you, as only if you are honest with them, can they make sure that they can give you the right kind of emotional, physical or informational support you need to enable you to focus on working through the therapy.

You may be tempted to skip a day of therapy or working on a particular technique, particularly if you are having a bad day, lack motivation or think that you don't have time. This will be disruptive to your focus and progress in the long term. Rather ensure that you stick with your plan and stay on track. Even if you don't feel like doing it a particular day, use one of the CBT techniques like Pleasant Activity Scheduling to help keep you focused and motivated. One of the benefits of the techniques and tools you learn through CBT is that they can be used to ensure you stay on track with committing to your goals for the therapy itself.

Real change takes time and you can't rush it. While you may see a few immediate positive changes, ongoing and lasting changes to your mindset and altering negative thinking patterns and automatic thoughts will take some time. You may find yourself seeing progress in one area and feeling worse in another. It is perfectly normal to hit a few stumbling blocks along away and you may even have days where you feel worse, not better. Understanding and identifying your negative thoughts can be an emotionally draining experience and at first, it may make you feel even worse about yourself and your problem. CBT is there to teach you how to move past those feelings and create new positive thoughts, feelings and emotions. Trust yourself and the process, and talk to someone if you feel overwhelmed.

As you work through the different techniques, either by yourself or with your therapist, you may have some homework that you will need to do in between sessions or activities. Part of CBT is to be able to put what you learn into practice, so you can start to see how your change in thinking is having a positive impact on your behavior and actions. You will only be able to see your progress and keep moving forward if you follow through on all the things you learn and actually do them. Remember, you need to practice in order to relearn, rethink and to grow and change.

Today could be the start of the rest of your life. Be brave enough to choose yourself and a better life for yourself. The cycle of negativity isn't one you need to be stuck in forever. You don't need to live a life filled with stress, anxiety and uncertainty. By learning the techniques, skills and tools that CBT can teach you, you are giving yourself an opportunity to start living the life you imagine. A life filled with positivity and hope; the life that you deserve and can have if you work toward it.

Leave the review

As an independent author with a small marketing budget, reviews are my livelihood on this platform. If you enjoyed this book, I'd really appreciate it if you left your honest feedback. I love hearing from my readers and I personally read every single review.

REFERENCES

7 Benefits of Cognitive Behavioral Therapy | CCPS. (2015, February 16). Comprehensive Consultation Psychological Services. http://comprehendthemind.com/7-benefits-cognitive-behavioral-therapy/

Ackerman, C. E. (2019, July 4). *25 CBT Techniques and Worksheets for Cognitive Behavioral Therapy*. PositivePsychology.Com. https://positivepsychology.com/cbt-cognitive-behavioral-therapy-techniques-worksheets/

Addiction Helper. (2012, November 16). *The different Types of Addiction and how they are related*. Addiction Helper. https://www.addictionhelper.com/addiction/types-of-addiction/

Akyurt, E. (2018). Sunset Women Model. In *Pixabay*. https://pixabay.com/photos/sunset-woman-model-pose-yoga-3726025/

Angeles. (2014). *Cognitive Behavioral Therapy Los Angeles*. Cognitive Behavioral Therapy Los Angeles. http://cogbtherapy.com/cognitive-behavior-therapy-techniques

Ankrom, S. (2019). *How to Breathe Properly for Relieving Your Anxiety*. Verywell Mind. https://www.verywellmind.com/abdominal-breathing-2584115

Boyes, A. (2012, December 6). *Cognitive Behavioral Therapy Techniques That Work*. Psychology Today. https://www.psychologytoday.com/za/blog/in-practice/201212/cognitive-behavioral-therapy-techniques-work

Brundt, A. (2019, June 3). *3 Steps to Treat Your Anxiety Using CBT*. Psychology Today. https://www.psychologytoday.com/za/blog/mindful-anger/201906/3-steps-treat-your-anxiety-using-cbt

CBT Therapy for Stress, ABCT. (n.d.). Www.Abct.Org. Retrieved July 21, 2020, from https://www.abct.org/Information/?m=mInformation&fa=fs_STRESS

Cherry, K. (2009, March 3). *Cognitive Behavioral Therapy*. Verywell Mind; Verywellmind. https://www.verywellmind.com/what-is-cognitive-behavior-therapy-2795747

Cherry, K. (2018). *Social Support Is Imperative for Health and Well-Being*. Verywell Mind. https://www.verywellmind.com/social-support-for-psychological-health-4119970

Clancy, C. (2019, August 8). *Treating Depression With Cognitive Behavioral Therapy - JourneyPure At The River*. JourneyPure At The River. https://journeypureriver.com/treating-depression-cognitive-behavioral-therapy/

Cognitive behavioral therapy - Mayo Clinic. (2017). Mayoclinic.Org. https://www.mayoclinic.org/tests-procedures/cognitive-behavioral-therapy/about/pac-20384610

Cuncic, A. (2020, June 29). *How to Change Your Negative Thought Patterns When You Have SAD*. Verywell Mind. https://www.verywellmind.com/how-to-change-negative-thinking-3024843

Daskal, L. (2016, June 22). 19 Highly Effective Ways to Stay Motivated. Retrieved August 26, 2020, from https://www.inc.com/lolly-daskal/19-simple-ways-to-stay-motivated-that-actually-work.html

Dickason, G. (2017). Alone Sad Depression. In *Pixabay*. https://pixabay.com/photos/alone-sad-depression-loneliness-2666433/

Flynn, H. A., & Warren, R. (2019, March 28). *Using CBT effectively for treating depression and anxiety*. Mdedge.Com.

https://www.mdedge.com/psychiatry/article/82695/anxiety-disorders/using-cbt-effectively-treating-depression-and-anxiety

Freepik. (2020). Back View Community. In *Freepik*. https://www.freepik.com/free-photo/back-view-community-young-people-united_6981839.htm#

FreePik. (2020). Flat lay of break bad habit concept. In *Free Pik*. https://www.freepik.com/free-photos-vectors/pencil">Pencil photo created by freepik - www.freepik.com

Fritscher, L. (2008, February 16). *The Role of Behavioral Therapy in the Treatment of Phobias*. Verywell Mind; Verywellmind. https://www.verywellmind.com/therapy-options-for-phobias-2672008

Fuller, J. R. (n.d.). *Cognitive Behavior Therapy - Types of CBT*. CBT Therapist NYC | NYC Psychologist | Dr. J. Ryan Fuller. Retrieved July 24, 2020, from https://jryanfuller.com/cognitive-behavior-therapy-cbt-types/#:~:text=Some%20forms%20of%20Cognitive%20Behavior

Gotter, A. (2018). *11 Ways to Stop a Panic Attack*. Healthline. https://www.healthline.com/health/how-to-stop-a-panic-attack

Gregoire, C. (2013, June 18). *5 Tricks From Cognitive Behavioral Therapy To Reduce Stress At Work*. HuffPost. https://www.huffpost.com/entry/managing-work-stress_n_3454501

Hain, J. (2015). Identity Self-Image. In *Pixabay*. https://pixabay.com/illustrations/identity-self-self-image-801212/

Halverson, J. (2018, February 28). *Cognitive Behavioral Therapy for Depression Technique: Approach Considerations, Behavioral Strategies, Initial Cognitive Strategies*. Emedicine.Medscape.Com. https://emedicine.medscape.com/article/2094696-technique#c3

Hartney, E. (2020, March 22). *Cognitive Behavioral Therapy For Addiction*. Verywell Mind. https://www.verywellmind.com/cognitive-behavioral-therapy-for-addiction-21953

Jacobson, S. (2011, April 3). *Cognitive Behavioral Therapy (CBT) for Phobias - What is it and Can it Help?* Harley TherapyTM Blog.

https://www.harleytherapy.co.uk/counselling/cognitive-behavioral-therapy-cbt-phobias.htm

Juergens, J. (2018, December 7). *Cognitive Behavioral Therapy - Addiction Center*. AddictionCenter. https://www.addictioncenter.com/treatment/cognitive-behavioral-therapy/

Kaczkurkin, A. N., & Foa, E. B. (2015). Cognitive-behavioral therapy for anxiety disorders: an update on the empirical evidence. *Dialogues in Clinical Neuroscience, 17*(3), 337–346. https://www.ncbi.nlm.nih.gov/pmc/articles/PMC4610618/

Koeck, P. (2015, May 25). *What is cognitive behavioral therapy in the treatment of stress?* 15 Minutes 4 Me. https://www.15minutes4me.com/stress-free/what-is-cognitive-behavioral-therapy-in-the-treatment-of-stress/

Legg, T. J. (2018, September 28). *Anxiety Exercises: 6 Exercises for Relief and Relaxation*. Healthline. https://www.healthline.com/health/anxiety-exercises

Legg, T. J. (2020, February 4). *Cognitive Restructuring: Techniques and Examples*. Healthline. https://www.healthline.com/health/cognitive-restructuring#finding-alternatives

Linforth, P. (2016). Anxiety Stress Depression. In *Pixabay*. https://pixabay.com/photos/anxiety-stress-depression-problem-2902575/

Linforth, P. (2017a). Hand Fear Despair. In *Pixabay*. https://pixabay.com/photos/hand-fear-despair-expression-2593743/

Linforth, P. (2017b). Stress Anxiety Depression. In *Pixabay*. https://pixabay.com/photos/stress-anxiety-depression-unhappy-2902537/

Martin, B., & read, P. D. L. updated: 19 J. 2019~ 14 min. (2016, May 17). *In-Depth: Cognitive Behavioral Therapy*. Psychcentral.Com. https://psychcentral.com/lib/in-depth-cognitive-behavioral-therapy/#:~:text=Cognitive%20behavioral%20therapy%20(CBT)%20is

Mikegi. (2020). Despair Sad Hand. In *Pixabay*.
https://pixabay.com/illustrations/despair-sad-hands-face-hood-cry-5237517/

Mind for Better Health. (2017, March). *About phobias*.
Www.Mind.Org.Uk. https://www.mind.org.uk/information-support/types-of-mental-health-problems/phobias/about-phobias/

Morrow, M. (2015). *CBT for Stress Management | KlearMinds*.
Klearminds. https://www.klearminds.com/therapies/cbt-cognitive-behavioral-therapy/stress/

Morrow, M. (2019, June). *CBT for Phobias*. Klearminds.
https://www.klearminds.com/therapies/cbt-cognitive-behavioral-therapy/phobias/

Pathak, N. (2018, February 09). Does Cognitive Behavioral Therapy
Treat Depression? Retrieved August 26, 2020, from
https://www.webmd.com/depression/guide/cognitive-behavioral-therapy-for-depression#1

Patterson, M. (2006). *CBT in Practice | Here to Help*.
Www.Heretohelp.Bc.Ca. https://www.heretohelp.bc.ca/cbt-practice

Phobia Treatment. (n.d.). Cognitive Behavioral Therapy Los Angeles.
http://cogbtherapy.com/phobia-treatment-los-angeles#:~:text=Cognitive%20behavioral%20treatment%20for%20phobias

Pixabay. (2017). Movement Work Clock. In *Pixabay*.
https://pixabay.com/photos/movement-work-clock-gears-face-2953852/

Polansky, B. (2019, October 10). *Cognitive Behavioral Therapy
Techniques for Addiction Recovery*. 1st Step Behavioral Health.
https://firststepbh.com/addiction-treatment/cognitive-behavioral-therapy-techniques/

Princing, M. (2019, September 9). *These At-home Cognitive Behavioral
Therapy Tips Can Help Ease Your Anxieties*. Right as Rain by UW
Medicine; RightAsRain.

https://rightasrain.uwmedicine.org/mind/stress/these-home-cognitive-behavioral-therapy-tips-can-help-ease-your-anxieties

Richards, T. A. (n.d.). *What is Cognitive-Behavioral Therapy? | The Anxiety Network*. Anxietynetwork.Com. https://anxietynetwork.com/content/cognitive-behavioral-therapy

Rupke, S. J., Blecke, D., & Renfrow, M. (2019). Cognitive Therapy for Depression. *American Family Physician, 73*(1), 83–86. https://www.aafp.org/afp/2006/0101/p83.html

Scott, E. (2020, February 7). *Cognitive Therapy Can Be Very Effective for Dealing With Stress*. Verywell Mind. https://www.verywellmind.com/cognitive-therapy-for-stress-relief-3144920

Serio, C. D. (2019, May 28). *Stop Negative Thoughts: Choosing a Healthier Way of Thinking | CS Mott Children's Hospital | Michigan Medicine*. Www.Mottchildren.Org. https://www.mottchildren.org/health-library/uf9857

Smith, M., Segal, R., & Segal, J. (2018). *Therapy for Anxiety Disorders: Cognitive Behavioral Therapy (CBT), Exposure Therapy, and Other Anxiety Treatments*. Helpguide.Org. https://www.helpguide.org/articles/anxiety/therapy-for-anxiety-disorders.htm

Soeiro, L. (2018, October 25). *Instant CBT: The Simplest Way to Challenge Negative Thoughts*. Psychology Today. https://www.psychologytoday.com/us/blog/i-hear-you/201810/instant-cbt-the-simplest-way-challenge-negative-thoughts

The American Institute for Cognitive Therapy - Home. (2009). Cognitivetherapynyc.Com. https://www.cognitivetherapynyc.com/stress.aspx

Therapist Aid, Treating Anxiety with CBT (Guide). (2012). *Treating Anxiety with CBT (Guide) | Therapist Aid*. Therapist Aid. https://www.therapistaid.com/therapy-guide/cbt-for-anxiety

Tracy, N. (2012, January 12). *Types of Addiction: List of Addictions |
HealthyPlace*. Healthyplace.Com.
https://www.healthyplace.com/addictions/addictions-information/types-
of-addiction-list-of-addictions

Tyrrell, M. (2016, March 7). *3 Instantly Calming CBT Techniques for
Anxiety*. Mark Tyrrell's Therapy Skills. https://www.unk.com/blog/3-
instantly-calming-cbt-techniques-for-anxiety/

Using Cognitive Behavioral Therapy (CBT) In Addiction Treatment.
(2020, April 30). Addiction Campuses.
https://www.addictioncampuses.com/addiction-treatment/cognitive-
behavorial-therapy/

Whalley, M. (2019, January 10). *Delivering more effective exposure
therapy in CBT | Psychology Tools*. Psychology Tools.
https://www.psychologytools.com/articles/delivering-more-effective-
exposure-therapy-in-cbt/

Why Self Help Doesn't Work | Life Change Support. (n.d.).
https://www.lifechangesupport.com/why-self-help-doesnt-work/

Wignall, N. (2019, April 8). *Cognitive Restructuring: The Complete
Guide to Changing Negative Thinking [2020]*. Nick Wignall.
https://nickwignall.com/cognitive-restructuring/

Williams, C., & Garland, A. (2002). A cognitive–behavioral therapy
assessment model for use in everyday clinical practice. *Advances in
Psychiatric Treatment, 8*(3), 172–179.
https://doi.org/10.1192/apt.8.3.172

9 798554 839948